# Psychosynthesis
# Made Easy

# Psychosynthesis Made Easy

### A psychospiritual psychology for today

Stephanie Sorrell

BOOKS

Winchester, UK
Washington, USA

First published by O-Books, 2011
O-Books is an imprint of John Hunt Publishing Ltd., Laurel House, Station Approach,
Alresford, Hants, SO24 9JH, UK
office1@o-books.net
www.o-books.com

For distributor details and how to order please visit the 'Ordering' section on our website.

Text copyright: Stephanie Sorrell 2010

ISBN: 978-1-84694-532-8

A CIP catalogue record for this book is available from the British Library.

Design: DKD

Printed in the UK by CPI Antony Rowe
Printed in the USA by Offset Paperback Mfrs, Inc

We operate a distinctive and ethical publishing philosophy in all
areas of our business, from our global network of authors to
production and worldwide distribution.

# CONTENTS

# ACKNOWLEDGEMENT

Without my years of training at the London Institute of Psychosynthesis, I would not have written this book. No work, book or training school could have created such solid ground to stand on. Particularly, I have found this psychospiritual psychology, founded by Psychiatrist, Roberto Assagioli, crucial in making sense of myself and the world. Thank you Roger Evans for always being there to lend advice and support my work. Your ability to teach with humor, sincerity and compassion is exemplary. Thank you also to my tutor, Anne Welsh, for being eternally optimistic of the direction I am going.

Without Hanne Jahr, my loyal friend, who painstakingly proof reads, suggests and constructively criticizes, I would fall short.

Thank you for your input on subpersonalities.

Thank you Janice Savage for your long hours of reading drafts and proofs. You rarely miss a thing !

# INTRODUCTION

Psychosynthesis is classified as a transpersonal psychology which became popular in the 1970s, when psychiatrists like Abraham Maslow and Carl Jung's work came to the fore. From the 1960s onward, it was a natural development to include the transpersonal dimension in the psychological field.

Our western understanding of psychology has grown from the bottom upwards; emerging from the roots of Behaviorism, through to Psychoanalysis, Cognitive Therapy and Humanistic Psychology which was already reaching out to embrace the transpersonal.

Although the ground level is important for any discipline, there is a point when it needs to grow and develop into its full potential. Up until Jung had come in with his theory of the 'collective unconscious' and Maslow brought in the reality of 'peak experiences', the spiritual aspect of psychology was not really credited with any value. Rather, it was seen to take energy away from a client's inner process when dealing with past trauma and send them into what is sometimes termed 'spiritual flight.' This was why Assagioli insisted that ego development was an important part of preliminary training and development. Although psychosynthesis is held within the matrix of the spiritual, it still emphasizes the importance of a good foundation in ego psychology. For example, if emerging therapists have not dealt with their own historical wounds which, very often, become the reason they want to be a counselor in the first place, the therapist's boundaries are too weak to enable clients to find their own boundaries.

Psychosynthesis is unique in that it places emphasis on the Self, the spiritual aspect of our makeup, as well as the self, the personality. This personal self individualizes to become the conscious 'I' when it makes choices and becomes self-aware as defined in the *egg diagram*. The transpersonal Self is able to perceive the vast area of untapped potential within the client. Building on this context is the potential of relationship which includes the client's relationship with themselves (intrapsychic) which will impact on the ability to form relationship with others in the world (interpersonal). The potential for relationship will be explored in the therapy room, not just in the client's relationship with the world, but in the dyadic connection with the therapist. I explore this further in the chapter, *The Power of Right Relationship.*

The other unique component of psychosynthesis is known as the *Disidentification Exercise* which is used extensively throughout the training both for clients and those undergoing training. By using this simple exercise consistently, either at the beginning of the day or when feeling overwhelmed by too many demands or influenced by someone's powerful emotional energy, the ability to 'disidentify' from circumstances becomes more accessible.

Before I came into psychosynthesis, I found that there were areas of my life that I had scarcely looked at, although I had been in and out of counseling through most of my 20s and 30s. Emotionally, I felt I had little or no control over my feelings so that again and again I found myself collapsing into them. I knew I had a strong will to persevere but I didn't know how to manage these powerful emotions without cutting out my feelings and vanishing into a world of spiritual flight.

Similarly, until we begin to work with our often fragmented will, we cannot manage our feelings or thoughts because they tend to run rampant until it seems impossible to break free of them. For anyone who is creative or wanting to develop their potential in this area, psychosynthesis enables one to explore this vast untouched area of ourselves through using imagery, symbols and visualization exercises which are so much a part of psychosynthesis.

It has been said that psychosynthesis resonates with the level of the heart, whereas encounter groups often only activate the solar plexus. As time goes by, and we become more spiritually and psychologically aware, the mind and heart begin to work together to realize a vision or work of value. More than anything, psychosynthesis holds the potential to move us from a position of little or no choice, to one of will and integration. At some point, we realize that taking responsibility for our lives, rather than blaming it on past and present outside conditions, becomes empowering rather than belittling.

An important maxim of Assagioli's which has great significance today, was the value of including the natural environment in the psychotherapeutic field. In the 1970s he wrote: *One might say an increasingly conscious sense of this universal brotherhood is behind the growing trend toward the cultivation of harmonious relations with the environment. This is the higher and broader aspect of ecology.* At the turn of the century an ecological awareness has increased along with the increasing necessity of endeavouring to protect what is fast becoming a diminished environment. Assagioli 's work was inevitably developing beyond preoccupation with the personality to the expansion of consciousness into the greater Self.

# CHAPTER 1

## Roberto Assagioli, the Psychiatrist

True to his pioneering nature, Roberto Assagioli was years ahead of his time. As the young Italian medical doctor and psychoanalyst emerged into the exciting world of the early 19th century, he was already riding in the wake of some influential and well established psychiatrists and thinkers.

Carl Jung was practising analytical psychology in Zurich, and Sigmund Freud working and teaching in the field of psychoanalysis in Vienna. Simultaneously, breakthroughs in inventive thought were happening in other areas of scientific interest. Einstein was working on his theory of relativity. Austrian philosopher, Rudolph Steiner, following a background in theosophy, became involved in founding the Anthroposophical Society in Germany. Its principal aims were in furthering the study of spiritual science.

The American Wright brothers had built the first manned plane and flown in it. Henry Ford had invented the T Model car. Additionally, new ideas were taking off in the artistic arena with the founding of the literary Bloomsbury group, a flamboyant and talented network of characters such as Virginia Woolf, Lytton Strachey, Lady Ottoline Morrell and Bertrand Russell.

But soon after Jung had enthusiastically recommended Assagioli to Freud, Roberto's initial ardor for the psychodynamic theory with its repressive elements in the unconscious waned. With hindsight, he saw the limitations of this model in that it failed to encompass the 'whole' human being. If all states of awareness could be attributed to past experience that had become unconscious, how could the inherent potential be harnessed in a human being?

Already, Assagioli's vision was extending towards unearthing the wealth of talent that was endeavouring to emerge within the client. He understood how easily the client could become trapped in the past. His own historical background had opened his awareness to the creative and spiritual qualities waiting to be tapped and harnessed within each human being. But in order to reach an understanding of Assagioli's unique psychological practice it is important to include here the forces that underpinned his formative years. His mother was both Jewish and a theosophist with a circle of friends who shared a keen interest in esoteric as well spiritual teachings.

As an Italian scholar, the young Roberto was introduced to Dante's *Divine Comedy which* formed a mandatory part of his education. This had impressed him deeply. In fact, when he had completed his training as a psychiatrist and broadened his practice, Dante's work was to form the bedrock of his own beliefs. Further, Roberto fully identified with the 13th century poet who was imprisoned and exiled from Florence, his homeland, for the last twenty years of his life. Ironically, at one point Assagioli's own life was endangered as a Jew during the Second World War and he too was imprisoned and exiled for a brief period for his political beliefs. But, more than anything, he saw *The Divine Comedy* as a complete metaphor for the spiritual journey and, indeed, referred to it as 'a wonderful picture of a complete psychosynthesis'. He equated the descent into the personality depths as *Hell*, or the *Abyss*, and then the aspiration towards transforming the lower aspects of the personality as *Purgatory*. Finally, as the 'I' achieved union with the Self, the soul would enter into *Paradise*.

Yet, despite his early coaching in esoteric matters, Assagioli felt it was important to develop his practice as a scientific psychology which 'encompassed the whole of man'. This psychology was to include creativity and will, as well as the often unconscious impulses and drives. Above all, he wanted his psychology to be practical and accessible to those who were drawn to the psychospiritual aspect of human development. Because of his background, he felt that this psychology should encompass the soul which could be used as a tool for *self-development* rather than *self-analysis*. He was not alone in holding the scientific context for his work. Both Jung and Freud had a similar need to do this. Indeed, Jung's fear of not being taken seriously did not allow his 'deeper' writings to be released until after his death.

Roberto Assagioli was to develop a close relationship with Alice Bailey, a spiritual teacher, who wrote a number of esoteric books on humanity's spiritual development. She shared his concern and interest for the psychosocial problems in the world, realizing that both global conditions and individual problems were inexorably compounded together. He was keen to share his knowledge with others and set up various education establishments in his own country and throughout the world.

Roberto shared a love of mountaineering with other thinkers such as Nietzsche and Ruskin, which can be a compelling metaphor for their preoccupation with developing the latent potential lying within humanity. He used the mountain as a model for our relationship with the superconsciousness in his work.

Assagioli was naturally interested in the Kabbalah, an esoteric and mystical component of the Jewish tradition in which his spiritual life was embedded. In his work he would refer to a period of great inner struggling in which all meaning seemed to be lost, sometimes known as the 'Dark Night of the Soul' or the 'abyss'. In the Kabbalah the 'abyss' precedes the final crossing from duality to Oneness. It is the 'Dweller on the Threshold' and what theosophist, Madam Blavatsky, described as something we have to confront whenever we entered a new threshold of inner and outer experience. In the abyss a great demon called Choronzon is encountered. He is the arch demon of false knowledge. To cross the abyss we need to leave all that we have known behind which is the task facing the initiate on the spiritual path.

Assagioli asserted that the whole purpose of dis-ease was to unpack the problems making up this dynamic and bring it into a spiritual context. He believed that the anxiety and psychological problems we suffer as individuals were an effort to achieve synthesis of the whole being, and the purpose of therapy was to foster this integration. In this context, problems become *opportunities* to achieve greater integration and self-awareness.

Because Assagioli understood the importance of being grounded in the world, he would treat the 'whole' person, initially using his training in psychoanalysis to locate hidden blocks in the personality. As we shall see in the chapter on *Subpersonalities* many of the blockages are developed in early childhood. This is not necessarily because parents are inherently bad but because they were emotionally handicapped in some way, performing their actions unconsciously as, perhaps, their own parents had done. Rather than blaming our ancestral lineage for being emotionally unaware, we need to remind ourselves that before the early 19th century there was very little opportunity to concentrate on psychological issues as the often physically onerous way of life did not leave room for this. The physical work of earning a living, putting bread on the table and caring for big families where there was little money available, took its toll on the body. Initially, it was only the wealthy and upper classes who had the money and time to explore the deeper issues of the unconscious. Indeed, many of Freud's clients were women from the upper classes who had time and money to give attention to what was going on in their unconscious and this we can be grateful for, because their experience laid the ground in psychoanalysis.

In the next chapter we will look at psychosynthesis alongside other psychologies that were emerging in the field. Although it is easy to look at one particular psychology in isolation, they are all uniquely embedded and developing out of each other like Russian dolls. We take time to look at the history of psychology and see how these have informed and influenced psychosynthesis.

# CHAPTER 2

## A Brief History of Preceding and Contemporary Psychologies

To see where Psychosynthesis stands in the arena of psychology we need to include the other major players in the field which preceded Psychosynthesis. These are commonly termed as the *three forces.*

Behaviorism, or the scientific study of behavior was defined as the *first force.* This was developed by a psychologist, Skinner, who with Pavlov, taught pigeons to walk in a figure of eight and dogs to salivate at the sound of a bell. The learning process had various names such as 'shaping behavior' which was developed by creating a reward system called behavior modification. Although developed in the early part of the 20th century, it proved a very popular method to use in mental health institutions. Despite its limitations in concentrating solely on behavior and not considering thoughts or feelings, its success certainly persisted into the 1970s when I was a student working with people with learning disabilities. Rewards in the form of sweets were given for good behavior and 'time out' or ignoring the person in question for negative unwanted behavior. Today, we still practise this in dog training with a positive or no reward system. Later, when Behaviorism developed into Cognitive Behavior Therapy( CBT), this became extremely popular because it had specific results. Unlike psychoanalysis, it did not try to uncover the reasons *why* a particular behavior persisted but instead drew up a plan with distinct stages to change patterns of negative or destructive thinking.

For example, a condition like agoraphobia could be addressed by a sequence of progressive stages over a period of 6-12 weeks with the support of a therapist. Because of its efficacy in appealing to the concrete mind, it was readily accepted by the government in 2007 as a highly effective way of treating depression. For this purpose a budget of 173 million was set aside to train over 3000 extra therapists in CBT.

Although it can be effective for treating depression caused by faulty thinking, it has not always been an effective tool in treating major or clinical depression where medication can be equally or more effective. Depression is still increasing, and as a senior psychologist confided in me: 'It certainly doesn't appear to be going away.'

The *second force* was applied to Psychoanalysis which was developed by Sigmund Freud and involved working with the unconscious. He believed that negative behavior patterns were determined by unconscious processes. These were sourced in the childhood in response to faulty early childhood development or traumas in the form of relationships with parental figures and siblings. He initiated the concept of 'ego development' which is still used today in childhood and, indeed, adult psychology. He theorized that the ego consisted of three parts, which occupy much of the unconscious. The young infant first develops what Freud referred to as the *Id*, full of powerful needs which cannot always be met. By the age of three, the child develops an *ego*, where the child learns that he is not the centre of his world. He is dependent on other people who have needs of their own. The ego is known as the *reality principle* informing the needy *Id* that it is not always possible to have what it wants immediately. At about five, the *superego* forms which is the conscience of the child. The ego basically does most of the work; moving between the id and the superego to make life easier for everyone.

Another important component developed by Freud was the process of *transference* and *countertransference*. Freud discovered this when he became aware that his clients were idealizing him by making him into something they wanted him to be, rather than what he was. Later, he found this transference very helpful in determining where the client was in their psychological process. Transference is where the client may transfer feelings they may have held for a significant person from their past onto the therapist. These are usually highly attractive feelings and cause the client to idealize the therapist.

The counter-transference is an energetic field which the therapist picks up from the client and will give him a clue as to what is going on in the psyche of his client. In the past, needy clients would project idealistic feelings onto the therapist and the therapist would sometimes respond to the seductive element and often a fated relationship would be acted out between the therapist and the client. This is different from the element of *projection* which are generally ambivalent feelings towards the therapist from the client who 'projects' someone from their past onto them.

A good humanistic or transpersonal therapist will be able to pick this up by being aware of the feelings in the room and how they themselves experience being an object of desire or ambivalence. The ability to perceive the transference in whatever form it may take is called the counter transference. To be the object of transference and projection is an important requirement in the therapeutic relationship as this allows these often unconscious feelings to be explored and made conscious in a safe environment.

Psychoanalysis and ego development form the bedrock of psychology and are an essential foundation in training for anyone wanting to be a Psychosynthesis counselor or psychotherapist.

Psychologist,Melanie Klein developed 'Object relations' from her practice working with small children and observing their relationship with their toys. Briefly, object relations are where the child's internalized world with siblings and parental figures is acted out through their toys or objects. Following on from this, this dynamic can be acted out in a wider environment where people will become objects belonging to past history, rather than the people they are in the present.

*The third force* was known as humanistic psychology. Although it was said to emerge in the 1950s, its roots are embedded in the older tradition of the healer/ shaman, who treated the whole person rather than the parts. The main founder here was American psychologist, Abraham Maslow, the 'spiritual father' of humanistic psychology.

It is interesting that Maslow started out as an enthusiastic behaviorist but became increasingly disillusioned by its reductive approach, where real people ceased to be people. Latterly, he became deeply critical of the somewhat reductionist and mechanistic psychologies of psychoanalysis and behaviorism. More and more, he found himself concentrating on looking at the whole person, rather than the parts. While Behaviorism and Psychoanalysis focused on what was *wrong* with the client, Maslow focused on the *positive aspects* of the personality like a basic goodness and creativity. He believed these positive aspects were inherent in all individuals, although they may have gone underground through trauma, they could be coaxed into the foreground through acceptance and trust.

Maslow went on to devise a hierarchy of needs that had to be attained before self- actualisation could occur. This hierarchy of needs worked from the bottom up from physiological needs, security needs, and belonging needs, esteem needs to self-actualisation. The individual could gain greater autonomy and become creative through having their basic needs met. We all know that when we enter a group situation we have an inherent need to feel safe, to belong.

*Maslow's Pyramid*

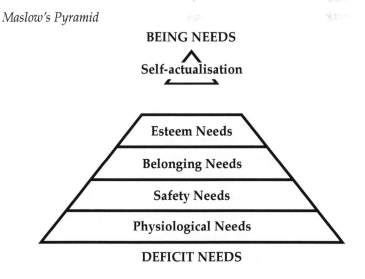

**BEING NEEDS**

**Self-actualisation**

**Esteem Needs**

**Belonging Needs**

**Safety Needs**

**Physiological Needs**

**DEFICIT NEEDS**

Self-actualization is the point where people become fully functional and able to realize their potential. Self-actualization is the basic force that drives the person forward. When a person is achieving their potential, then they have what Maslow termed as a 'peak experience'. This is an experience which transcends the ego boundaries and where the subject comes in touch with their full potential. This can manifest as spiritual realisation, but not necessarily a religious one. Self-actualization is the desire and drive to becoming everything we are capable of becoming.

Maslow believed that we should study and cultivate peak experiences as a way of providing a route to achieve personal growth, integration and fulfillment. Peak experiences are unifying and ego-transcending: bringing a sense of purpose and integration to the individual. Individuals most likely to have peak experiences are self-actualized, mature, healthy, and self-fulfilled. All individuals are capable of peak experiences. Those who do not have them may, through fear, suppress or deny them. This is sometimes known as 'repression of the sublime' and can plunge the subject into a deep depression as they are denying their innermost nature. In a sense, this is soul betrayal.

Maslow carried out a study of self-actualizers throughout history and within contemporary society. He identified a number of characteristics they all had.

- **Accepting of themselves and others**
- **More efficient in perceiving reality**
- **More spontaneous in their relationships**
- **Tendency to focus on the solutions to problems rather than the problems themselves**
- **An autonomy from cultural influences and societal injunctions**
- **A capacity for transcendence/intense mystical experiences**
- **A deep identification with humanity with empathy**
- **A sense of humor**

- **Ability to be creative**

This development in psychology was inevitably going to give rise
to transpersonal psychology where it followed on the heels of peak
experiences. This I shall address next.

## Transpersonal Psychology

The transpersonal theorists understood the importance of building
a healthy ego in order to ground the insights that were accessible
from the superconscious. The problem is not so much in believing
that we are primarily a spiritual being living in a physical body,
but in *understanding* one's psychological strength and weaknesses
enough to deal with this insight. For example, it was not by chance
that in the Jewish mystical tradition of the Kabbalah, students were
not accepted into the study of the Tree of Life until they were 40 or
were at least married. This was so that the potential student's insight
could be properly grounded in the world, enabling a strengthening
of self through facing the rigors of life. Conscious dedication to the
spiritual path is never an easy choice, although it may sometimes be
seen as a means of escape.

Although Carl Jung, Roberto Assagioli, Charles Tart, Stanislav
Grof and Ken Wilber have become richly associated with developing
transpersonal psychology, Maslow and his work on self-actualization
and peak experiences was one of the original pioneers.

Additionally, Charles Tart, Professor of Psychiatry at the
University of California and lecturer in Psychology at Stanford
University, has been one of the leading researchers and proponents
in transpersonal psychology. He defines transpersonal psychology
as going beyond the ego which represents the reality principle.
Good at posing key questions which open up awareness, he asks;
'Why would anyone want to go beyond the ego if this is our link
with reality? Is it to escape the confines of a reality that has become
unbearable or to look for further meaning?'

He believed that the fundamental preoccupation for those

interested in transpersonal experiences was a need to inject a new sense of purpose into their lives; one that would redefine the meaning of their life experience.

Under the heading of 'transpersonal experience' are altered states of consciousness (ASC), out of the body experiences (OBEs), peak experiences, unidentified flying object encounters (UFOs) and spontaneous healing. All these impact on the psyche in such a way that there is a profound change in inner values and perspective.

Deep values, Tart perceived, really come from an intense personal experience. Consequently, once a sense of purpose is activated, life becomes pregnant with value and meaning. This can be true for founders of a particular religion or spiritual faith where they have experienced some intense personal contact with a spiritual insight or truth in the form of a vision or teaching. This is both experiential and energetic and attracts others to itself. But as time passes, and the magnetism that initially drew people to the 'truth' becomes watered down, the sense of aliveness that animated the work diminishes. In time, the rational scientific mind dismisses it as nonsense; a set of superstitions that have outlived their usefulness. Unless a spiritual insight initiates a technology of practice for its followers to carry out in the form of meditation, prayer and visualization, the religion or truth cannot sustain itself. Practice is as important as the original core teaching. It sustains the insight and strengthens the connection. This is true for all the major religions which firmly encourage diligent and regular practice.

One of Charles Tart's preoccupations was to build bridges between science and religion rather than maintain the splits. He highlighted the need for both scientists and mystics to bridge the split that separates the two by fostering a sense of humility. Humility counteracts the danger of arrogance that arises in both the mystic, the one who has had the transpersonal experience and the scientist who defends himself strongly against anything that can threaten his mindset. Humility, he believed, opens the door to true dialogue between the two, whereas arrogance keeps the door locked and barred. He writes, "The conflict is between second rate science and second rate mystics, between dogmatic people….. When people become psychologically attached to their beliefs, become defensive, and feel the need to attack other people's beliefs and conflict arises."

Unless there is openness to dialogue through one's insights rather than rushing to convert others, the transpersonal experience cannot be properly integrated. That is why it is so essential to have grounding in early ego development, or else one identifies with the transpersonal experience and becomes inflated, thinking, 'they are the one'. This is no good to anyone and can be dangerous if the experience becomes enmeshed with the ego. No transpersonal experience however profound can take the place of good grounding and healthy ego development.

'Psychosynthesis definitely affirms the *reality* of spiritual experience, the existence of the higher values' wrote Assagioli.

But Assagioli also believed that one did not have to be religious in order to have a spiritual experience. A spiritual experience might emerge from a religious conversion or inner vision, but spiritual experience is available to everyone regardless of their background or cultural beliefs. This experience may be standing in a field, watching the breeze combing through the blades of grass and the light catching it in a certain way that communicates with something deep inside us. It may be opening the window and smelling the first promise of spring or the sight of a butterfly or watching your child take its first step. In fact the spiritual experience may have nothing to do with any of these events in themselves, but can, instead, manifest through them.

In these moments the person understands that a sense of spirituality can emerge from contact with the superconscious where the 'I', which is a reflection of the Self, can be transported to this superconscious level, be it a piece of music, poetry or first love. There is a sense of being a part of something greater than oneself. With the infusion of superconsciousness the recipient may feel inspired to serve in some way in life, or even take a new career direction or, if one is artistic, paint or write a poem. We do not even have to be creative. The experience might inspire us to create a piece of artwork for the first time. Superconsciousness is accessible to everyone, irrespective of their class, religion or background. Certainly Bill Wilson, an alcoholic, came into touch with the superconsciousness and after that referred to it as his 'Higher Power'. In fact, Carl Jung had said to him when he asked for help that there wasn't much hope for release from his addiction if he did not believe in a power greater than himself. A power that was able to transform, heal and inspire one to a life of selfless service... The maxim of AA is; 'We came to believe that a Power greater than ourselves could restore us to sanity.' Bill Wilson was a living example of this in founding the world community, Alcoholics Anonymous.

Access to a heightened state of consciousness can be harnessed through meditation , prayer yoga or similar exercises. Conscious visualisation and meditation, in quieting the outer mind, increases ones receptivity to the Self, as does the Disidentification Exercise (chapter 5). Often, in the early stages of one's commitment to a spiritual life, through disillusionment or the need for meaning, value and purpose, one may experience a honeymoon spell. The recipient may feel as though they are basking in a superior state of consciousness and their life may become less of a struggle, effortless in a way. But this is literally a honeymoon and after this period the initiate's will and commitment is tested severely. The initiate finds themselves in a challenging place where there seems to be little help at hand and may have to journey deep inside themself to find the tools that they need to make any progress.

The next chapter looks at the Egg Model which is central to psychosynthesis as a complete model of consciousness.

# CHAPTER 3

## The Egg as a Model of Consciousness

If you have always wondered which came first, the chicken or the egg, the egg certainly comes first in psychosynthesis. In fact, although Assagioli only intended it as a temporary model of consciousness until he found something better to replace it, the egg's symbolism is still resonating loud and strong throughout training schools and seminars throughout the world. Its efficacy is in its innate simplicity in being a template for the levels of consciousness that make up the human being.

Consciousness is our area of direct awareness.

Unconsciousness consists of areas that exist within and outside us that may, through dreams, therapy or life trauma, emerge into consciousness in an effort to be recognized. Often, when there have been a series of traumatic events in one's life, the memory of these are repressed until we feel ready to deal with them. In this light, painful memories are repressed for our own survival and safety.

The collective unconsciousness exists outside our personal consciousness but, because all the lines dividing the areas of consciousness are semi permeable( see Egg Model), knowledge of what lies outside our direct awareness may seek to be acknowledged. Those of us who are more intuitive than others may have insight through dream content or periods of relaxation.

When a number of people simultaneously have the same idea for an invention, a work of art or a novel, they are tapping unconsciously into the collective unconsciousness. Although individuals may claim the idea was theirs, it may have been floating about in the collective unconscious until someone was ready to take it on. Similarly, many historical figures received their most well known insights through this medium of communication, like Einstein and his theory of relativity and Newton and his theory of gravity. Poets, musicians and writers may be in touch with the Self or transpersonal self for their inspiration. I want to include an example of when I encountered a case of someone tuning very accurately into the collective unconscious without realizing it. This man, Peter, was a professional artist whom I met on holiday. He would often display his paintings on his website. One particular scene had haunted him in a dream, so much so that he had painted it. The scene was of an aircraft hitting tall buildings. In the wake of the 11.11 disaster in the USA, Peter chose to close down his site. He was also extremely shaken by the event and his ability to pick up the event before it happened.

*The Egg Model*

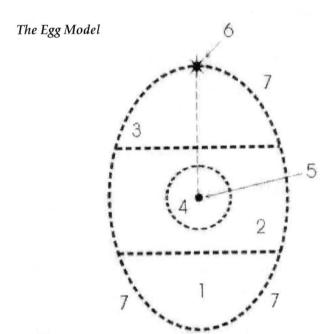

1. *The Lower Unconscious* represents the 'difficult' past, made up of subliminal drives, complexes and primitive urges that propel the personality towards achieving certain goals. Within this almost primeval soup lie phobias, obsessions and paranoid delusions and dream content of an 'inferior kind'. Even if a person experienced

a relatively easy childhood, there are bound to be incidents that occurred, even experienced through the television screen, a book, or snippets of conversation that may have been hard to process so that it is relegated to the unconscious content. If we identify strongly with these primitive drives, we can believe that they are all of us, rather than a part of consciousness with which we strongly identify.

2. *The Middle Unconscious* is much more accessible to everyday waking consciousness. This can be likened to liminal space where experiences are assimilated and waiting to emerge into awareness. This is the most immediate layer of unconscious material that is available to us. We can recall events that have impacted on us recently and bring them to light without much difficulty.

3. *The Higher Unconscious* is where we receive our intuition and highest creative and inspirational insights. When we are in touch with this area, our ethical conscience is awakened and there is a strong call to 'service'.

4. *The Field of Consciousness* is where our everyday awareness resides.

5. *The Conscious self* or 'I' is the centre of our being, a point of pure self-awareness and will. It is a reflection of the Self. It may be helpful to understand its capacity to reflect the best and worst around us, according to our level of consciousness. As we become more self-aware, we can learn to choose what we identify and disidentify with.

6. *The Self* is above and outside the stream of contents passing through everyday consciousness. It is that part of us that is unaffected by the everyday experiences of life. It can be equated to the Spirit. This is not to be confused with psychism which often becomes confused with the level of Spirit. The distinction that can

be made here is that the Self/Spirit is pure and contains less content than psychism which is more attached to the personality level where there is a lot of activity.

7. *The Collective Unconscious* is where one is impacted on by the changing contents of the 'sea' we are immersed in. The membrane that surrounds the egg is porous, allowing for 'psychological osmosis' to take place.

## Keeping the balance

Although the fundamental principle of psychosynthesis is that Self is an ontological being which is both transcendent and immanent, Assagioli warned against the tendency for students and practitioners in becoming too polarized towards self-realization. His background in psychodynamic psychology and the importance of developing a strong ego container, had taught him the importance of grounding. He saw that, because of painful historical trauma, there could be a tendency to split off from challenging material in the unconscious and an impulse to veer towards 'mystical flight'. He emphasized the importance of balance in all aspects of psychosynthesis and postulated that it was only in grounding insights and realizations that any true progress could be made.

He saw how the upper and lower aspects of the unconscious were complementary and worked together. Whatever was activated in the upper unconscious through meditation and visualization exercises would have an effect on the lower unconscious which could result in turbulence within the personality as various defence mechanisms holding unconscious material struggled to gain dominion. Always the Self was striving for greater union and harmony. Similarly, work on the level of the personality where the student is striving to harness challenging forces in his make-up, will affect the higher unconscious, bringing insight, strength and joy to the troubled personality.

This underscores the biblical maxim: 'As above, so below'

where the kingdom of heaven is not just reflected on the earth, but immanent therein.

For me, the egg is a model of potential. Like the organic egg belonging to the hen it has a whole life encapsulated within it.

Next we look at subpersonalities, which is unique to psychosynthesis and a way of exploring and understanding the many aspects of ourselves that largely operate unseen. Consciousness of our subpersonalities brings greater awareness and autonomy over our actions.

# CHAPTER 4

## Subpersonalities

*All the world's a stage and the men and women its players.*
*Each man and woman plays many parts, has its entrances and exits.*
**Shakespeare**

Shakespeare's well-known lines immediately came to mind when I first encountered the theme of subpersonalities. The reason these lines have resonated throughout history is because we understand inherently that this is true. In fact, it was William James who first referred to these 'heterogeneous personalities' as an explanation for the multi-faceted ways in which the personality expresses itself.

Assagioli took this a step further by developing his work on subpersonalities. He believed that these autonomous entities originated from the lower unconscious and formed in childhood in response to the conflicts going on in the early environment. Subpersonalities worked independently and remained with the child as it matured into an adult. He used his insight into subpersonalities in his work with clients by enabling them to become aware of their existence in their life. He believed that in learning to recognize them by identifying with them, one could then disidentify with them.

Most of us have aspects of ourselves which we would call the Clown, the Raver, the Critic, the Sneak, the Big Spender, the Skinflint, the Needy One, the Flirt and the Goodie-Goodie. Giving them a name helps us identify with them more; like Jealous Jennie or Selfish Simon. Understandably, we don't mind others seeing the more acceptable parts of ourselves because it earns us good kudos. But if we have a Sneaky Sandra or a Simon Skinflint we try to keep them hidden from others, enveloping them in shame and loathing which takes huge amounts of energy.

Supposing we have a part of us that enjoys joking around and making a fool of ourselves because it releases tension and makes us popular with others. Perhaps we can call this part of us ' Cal the Clown'. That's fine until Cyril the Critic comes along and dampens our mood. Immediately we feel chastened and ridden with guilt and slip out of our clown subpersonality. This happens time and time again every time we are relaxing and having a good time and then along comes Miserable Minnie who demands our attention too. What do we do when these subpersonalities become conscious? Can we continue allowing Cyril the Critic to keep sabotaging our fun and making us depressed?

In psychosynthesis, through visualization and dialogue, the therapist will try to resolve this dilemma by making these subpersonalities conscious. It is obvious that Cal the Clown wants to lighten things up, but why is Cyril the Critic being such a pain and making us so unhappy? Although the last thing we want to do is to face Cyril the Critic, we know that in order to move forward we need to know what he wants from us. Cyril the Critic, it turns out, is trying to look after us, by stopping us getting into trouble. Maybe humor was a difficult issue in the family constellation and it landed us in trouble. So then we ask what Cyril the Critic needs and he tells us that he wants our love and acceptance! Well – that's big coming from him when all he wanted to do was dampen our spirits! But then we dialogue with Miserable Minnie who tells us she likes both the clown and the critic but she is miserable because they are always at war with each other and she just wants them to be more tolerant of each other.

By recognizing the needs and wants of these subpersonalities, there is always the fear that if we give these subpersonalities more attention, they will take over. But in actuality, the opposite happens. Because the conflicting subpersonalities are seen and acknowledged and are conscious, they can negotiate with each other by 'time sharing'.

Another valid point here is this: If we can recognize these various subpersonalities, who is doing the observing?

And here we can return to the metaphor at the beginning of the article of the conductor with his orchestra. Basically, the 'I', our sense of 'I-ness' is the conductor. And ironically, the more subpersonalities we are conscious of, the stronger becomes our sense of 'I'. As we claim back these disparate parts of ourselves, the orchestra becomes more harmonious than before and we, in turn, become more autonomous beings.

In psychosynthesis these 'parts' which spring into action given the right underlying signals, like stress or threat, are subpersonalities which have been with us for so long that we don't question them. Their formation happened sometime in childhood when we felt threatened, exiled or punished by other children, teachers or even our parents. In a sense, they have served us well by being part of a survival mechanism. Because they are largely unconscious, they belong in the bottom part of the egg diagram, the lower unconscious. They only emerge into our field of consciousness if we are challenged by something or someone that activates old memories slumbering in the basement of our psyche.

From a psychosynthetic point of view, aspects of our personality are there for a reason and serve a purpose in getting us what we need, but maybe the intention behind the need has become distorted or lost. Once we can understand that all these subpersonalities at their core, behind their want, are looking for love and acceptance then the first stage of synthesis has begun. This first stage is called *recognition* as we are able to identify this part of us.

**Recognition**

It is impossible to change anything that we dislike about ourselves unless we are conscious of it. Ironically, we may be the last one to see that a troublesome subpersonality is running rampant in our life, although this may be clearly visible to everyone around us. A psychosynthesis therapist will, first of all, help us to be aware of our repetitive behavior that is keeping us locked in our history rather than moving forward. Through creative imagery exercises and developing the 'I', the observing component of our being, we can further become aware of it by giving it a name. Naming a 'behavior' makes it real and conscious. Naming the subpersonality is an act of taming it by making a connection with it, or owning it. The author, Ursula Le Guin writes about this in her 'Earthsea trilogy':

*Ged sighed sometimes, but he did not complain. He saw that in this dusty and fathomless matter of learning the true name of each place, thing, and being, the power he wanted lay like a jewel at the bottom of a dry well. For magic consists in this, the true naming of a thing.*

If we have suffered abuse or trauma to the psyche, identifying and naming the shame can be very freeing. It is as if 'speaking' the condition breaks the spell that has been cast in the unconscious. It no longer owns us. We are in control. Naming and owning literally breaks the ties that bind us to a behavior or person. In the therapy room, the client and therapist engage in 'speak healing'.

As what was unconscious becomes conscious by our *recognition* it moves up a level to the middle of the egg and into the direct sphere of the 'I' which is the observer. The key is in owning that part of ourselves. The wild child running amok in the basement of our unconscious has been given a name. This is the first step of synthesis. It does not need to be a wild child any more because the light of awareness is beginning to dawn: life has moved on. What threatened the child in the past is no longer there. The therapist, by helping the client to be aware of this, will enable the client to move on by navigating through boundaries of the past. Some people have worried about losing a subpersonality that they have grown rather attached to, even dependent on, yet nothing is really lost, but integrated instead.

**Acceptance**
The next step, which can take longer if there is too much resistance, is *accepting* this aspect of us. In our childhood, it served us well by helping us to survive by developing a false persona. As children, we do not have a lot of choice in the parts we play because it is all an effort

to survive in a challenging situation. As adults, there is the choice not to be ruled by unconscious elements which can work against us by stultifying further growth and development. Obviously, much of the work that brings us to this level of awareness is rooted in the early childhood environment. Once we can accept this part of ourselves it moves us forward to the next stage. Resistance or denial of this can be a heavy burden to bear because it keeps us imprisoned and unable to move forward and realize our full potential.

## Coordination

For integration between subpersonalities to take place, there must be a process happening *within* each subpersonality. Change can only happen when we recognize the strengths and weaknesses of each subpersonality and develop compassion and empathy for the challenging conditions that each subpersonality may have emerged from. Subpersonalities and their life are really an inner representation of the complexities existing in our social world. We might dislike various people and condemn their behavior. Yet – once we understand why they act as they do and that this was part of their survival mechanism, we can begin to *like* and *understand* them. We, literally, enter into Right Relationship (chapter 6) with them. Underneath the behavior that might have been aggressive or strange, is the desire to be loved and accepted. The behavior is a symptom of things that may have gone wrong historically. In this light, it is possible to see how by a process of coordination with our subpersonalities, we can improve relationships around us in society – or, at least we can understand why the behavior is there.

Subpersonalities do not live in isolation.

In fact, as work goes on in psychosynthesis a whole crew of seemingly disparate subpersonalities may struggle for recognition and acceptance. Some of these are familiar to most of us; James the judge. Henrietta, the hell-raiser, Charles the crusader and Freya the freedom lover! As our self-awareness increases we usually find that more and more subpersonalities keep popping up for recognition. It is rather like the lyrical 'old woman who lived in a shoe' who had so many children she did not know what to do!

Mid-life, the late 30s to mid 40s, is a crucial time for change; when we realize that time is slipping by and if we do not do all the things that we kept putting off because we were too scared, the whole opportunity will soon pass us by. If this awareness isn't able to become fully conscious, we reach a midlife crisis where there may be a period of new romances, a divorce, a new career, a major move, all with their emotional entanglements. These can become repeating patterns of behavior that may only become conscious through loss and heartache. By utilizing the power of therapy, both the therapist and client will draw up a plan to work together in an effort to locate what the subpersonalities *want* and *need*. The *want* might be for power and recognition, but underlying this will be a *need* for love and acceptance which might have been present from childhood. The more a subpersonality has navigated the first two stages of synthesis, the more ready we are to accept *all* these parts of us and, like a puppeteer, allow the various aspects to coordinate together. True acceptance is having compassion and understanding for these rejected parts of our psyche.

## Integration

Through the process of *integration*, we learn to synthesize these various aspects of our persona. In time, we learn to recognize subpersonalities for what they are and are less concerned about how to get rid of them or control them, but rather respect the role they have played in our formative years. Subpersonalities create character and this like a fingerprint is valuable because it is a record of our inner development. Really our collection of subpersonalities are components of a magnificent orchestra, each sounding their own note. But as time goes by and we are able to work with these aspects of ourselves, the orchestra changes as subpersonalities move in and out of the foreground.

## Synthesis

Synthesis is the final stage of the work with subpersonalities. It is a culmination of all the other stages. But, as with anything organic, it is not an end in itself. As long as we are here on earth we are learning and growing and our inner work is never really finished.

*Exercise for finding your subpersonalities*

The following exercise is used in psychosynthesis initially to locate our subpersonalities, and can be repeated at intervals to see which may be prominent at a particular time.

*Imagine yourself walking through a meadow of wild grasses threaded through with meadowsweet. Experience the sense of freedom around you....*

*Directly ahead of you is a white cottage with a thatched roof. Feeling drawn to it, you walk up the cobbled garden path and knock on the door because you know that inside there are people you have been wanting to meet.*

*Be aware of the person who answers the door and invites you in. What do they look like? Are they young or old? What do they say to you?*

*Stepping inside, several people come to meet you. What are they like? Do they have anything to say to you? How do you feel in response?*

*One of them leads you downstairs to the basement. Be aware of any visceral thoughts and feelings. Perhaps there is someone there who has been waiting for you to visit for some time. What do they look like? Do they have a name? Do you have anything to say to them? What do you feel?*

*Perhaps the character who let you into the house invites you to meet more people upstairs who may be familiar to you. What do these people look like? What do you have to say to each other? Perhaps, if you look through the windows outside, you can see the garden below with more people waiting to greet you. Decide whether you want to meet them yet, knowing that you will have many opportunities to return and do so. What is the landscape like outside the window?*

When you withdraw from the visualization and return to your present age, it is worth making notes of your experience as you will need this to refer to later on in your work.

The levels of the house represent the levels within us, with some areas more accessible and inviting than others. Know that you can go back to this cottage anytime in your active imagination to meet these aspects of yourself which will lend insight into your personality

# CHAPTER 5

## The Disidentification Exercise

*We are dominated by everything with which our self becomes identified.*
*We can dominate and control everything from which we*
*disidentify ourselves.*
***Assagioli***

This is the most important exercise in Psychosynthesis. Do not be misled by its apparent simplicity. The efficacy and beauty of this exercise lies in its simplicity. Once we can grasp Assagioli's words, that 'we are dominated by everything we identify with', we are in possession of a life changing knowledge. But just think about this for a few minutes:

*We are dominated by everything with which our self becomes identified!*

In fully acknowledging this, we can consistently apply this to our thoughts and feelings. The next task is to be aware of it as you go about your daily rituals, work, interests, errands and hobbies. Be especially vigilant as you read the local newspaper and nonchalantly watch the television adverts in the evening that seem to invariably focus on food and holidays. Be aware of visceral reactions to chocolate adverts and holidays that seem to want to sweep you up and deliver you seamlessly to that caster sugar-coated shore. How do you manage these temptations? Do you reach for the chocolate you've been trying to restrain yourself from diving into? Do you find yourself mentally calculating where and when to plan your next holiday until the reality of dwindling funds noses its way into reality? Perhaps you find yourself juggling with the upgrade to the bathroom or a newer car model. With the bigger things, common sense tends to kick in, but it is the smaller items that we find less able to resist, which whittle away at our will power.

For example, you are working on the computer, doing spreadsheets, planning out a timetable or writing an article or email. You are a little bored and you can't be bothered to leave the room to make a coffee, but then there's an audible 'plop' into your digital mail box. You come out of the program, see that it's a marketing piece from Amazon and not from anyone you know. But, even so, you just decide to take a peek because you are always interested in books. You scan through, past the books and they're offering a 50% reduction on laptops, just because you had a bored little browse yesterday. You pan in and there's a laptop which could serve you well with a lot more working memory and, since your old PC has been crashing and freezing for the last two months, this would be a worthwhile investment.

If we have any sense, we will be able to disidentify enough to take a step back, return to our work and let some time pass. All sales people know that if they don't seize their prey in the first few minutes, the opportunity is lost.

Later, there might be a follow up from Amazon on the heels of this in the hope of ensnaring your will again and if your computer keeps freezing, the temptation may give way to a genuine need to buy 'that' laptop. The beauty of online advertising is that your email is always available 24 hours a day. And you don't have to get into the car or write a letter to place an order. You just press a few buttons.

Identification is key here. We cannot disidentify from what we are not conscious of. But identification is more than fashion accessories and food. It is education, politics, the environment, our job and career, foreign affairs, our animals, the pub, jogging, along with our many hobbies like gardening and bicycling. These identifications, whatever form they take, are like kites in our hands that pull us into their world from time to time to follow their direction. Identification is where we place our meaning, purpose and value, which is good on one level, because we all need this. But, on a negative level, it is where we are *most* caught, addicted even.

Perhaps, as you are reading this, you may find yourself becoming a little defensive, embarrassed or humored by the intensity of your interests. When we strongly identify with something or someone, we also feel emotional about them.

However, this is not so much about giving up our interests as taking responsibility for them and the amount of time we spend on them in contrast with other activities. Becoming aware of who and what we are strongly identified with gives us a certain power of choice and clarity. Because when we let go of our identification, we are free to allow something 'more' into our consciousness, the transpersonal even. Creativity, which is the grist behind any work of art, is key to this. Inspiration often steps in when the 'I' identifies with the Superconsciousness. To be free to create, there needs to be a certain amount of disidentification from all the 'kites' which can pull our energy away from putting this into practice. Although the potency of the exercise is in its simplicity, it cannot be rushed.

To carry this out effectively, we need to close our eyes against outside distraction and become aware of our breathing. Following this, we make a conscious effort to slowly breathe our way into our body. Be aware of bodily sensations such as aches, tiredness, tension. Accept these sensations and release them, then acknowledge:

*I **have** a body, but **I am not** my body*
Next, let this go and pan into your emotional life. Acknowledge negative emotions such as disappointment or positive ones such as expectancy and happiness. Then let them go as you breathe out and affirm:

*I **have** an emotional life, but **I am not** my emotions or feelings*
Be aware now of your thoughts and ideas. These may be preoccupations with world news, the workplace, family or marital issues. Accept them, and then as you make a decision to let them go, breathe out and affirm:

*I **have** a mind, but **I am not** my mind*

Now take a few moments to become aware of yourself as a point of consciousness and you might find it easier to focus on a point in the middle of your forehead, just above and between your eyebrows. This corresponds to a centre of meditational attunement in many Eastern and Yogic exercises. Just do what feels comfortable to you. As you breathe out affirm the final part of the exercise:

*I am a center of pure consciousness and Will*
Rest in this knowledge for a while and experience the peace in being here now.

## Clarifying Disidentification
Here, I want to affirm that disidentication is not the same as *dissociation*, where there is often an unconscious cutting off from thoughts, memories and images because they are too disturbing to hold. Yet Carl Jung believed dissociation can be a need to cut off from outside influences in order to concentrate on an important creative or educational work. The distinction is in the conscious and unconscious choice between the two. The inclusion of both identification and disidentification allows us to move onto the next component of the exercise. For example, if we are angry or irritable, we cannot successfully disengage ourselves from their influence unless we acknowledge them first. If we dissociate from them, rather than dis-identify with them, they rule us unconsciously instead. Assagioli's famous quote was 'what we deny, rules', rings true here. What has been exiled, may not rule us from center stage, but it will rule us from the wings, draining energy away from performing our full potential. This is reminiscent of Jung's words too 'what we resist, persists'.

It is important, when beginning this exercise, to keep a journal as an ongoing record of your inner process. Because you are effectively changing the habits of a life time where you may not have been aware of your conscious thought, let alone made an effort to observe it, progress can be slow. But, rather like water dripping onto stone, you will make headway as the observing 'I' part of you moves from background to foreground.

Many therapists and health practitioners make use of this exercise in their work and it can also be utilized as a prelude to meditation. If our body, mind and feelings are all jostling for attention, then the prospect of finding peace and insight through meditation can be almost impossible.

By beginning one's day with the disidentification exercise, whether at a desktop computer or creating some psychological space before everyone else gets into work, there is a sense of peace and detachment from all the pressures weighing heavily upon us. Because this exercise connects with the body, heart, mind level before identifying with a centre of pure consciousness, it is both grounding and expansive.

Throughout my four years of training, each morning session would begin with this exercise and as I sat there after an hour and a half trek across London in rush hour, I experienced a great peace within my soul and a sense of coming home to my self.

In the next chapter we look at the significance of being in right relationship with the world, each other and our innermost self. Also we, briefly, explore the energy of group work in a smaller family context and within the larger group of society.

# CHAPTER 6

## The Power of Right Relations and Group Work

*In actual life a relationship is always present, recognized or unrecognized, conscious or unconscious. The individual is never absolutely alone and God (or the spiritual reality) is never purely transcendent. But always in living relationship with the manifestation.*
**Roberto Assagioli**

One of the key principles of psychosynthesis is the focus on relationship. This is both interpersonal relationships which is the relationship we have with each other, and intrapersonal relationship, the relationship which we have with ourselves. If we are out of relationship with ourselves, for example through conflict or faulty mindsets, we may unconsciously use these as lenses to perceive the 'other' through. For example, if through our early relationship with our mother, we felt unable to express ourselves because our emotional way of expression was unacceptable, we would allow this to eclipse our communication with others, especially older women. This could impact on our work or social situations where we would feel uncomfortable with older female figures and may use old and outworn patterns of behavior to affect our relationship with them. To compensate for this early wounding, we might approach older female figures in an arrogant or defensive way, or crave their affection instead.

Although accepting that our negative history may not make future relationships any the less challenging, conscious awareness will give us the ground to make choices between collapsing into old and outworn behaviors or choosing to behave differently. We can choose to develop a different way of 'meeting' the other person, rather than reacting to our own personal history.

This awareness of relationship may begin in the therapy room with the therapist who will help identify and unearth mindsets that are no longer serving us or are undermining our ability to move forward in certain areas of our life. Being able to explore different ways of behaving and reacting to our therapist creates a safe environment where we can practise different ways of behaving. It is true that change within us, in turn, impacts on our wider relationship with the world in the form of the other person.

Other obstacles which undermine our ability to have a right relationship with others are cultural ones which need to be learned or unlearned. We may also have assumptions and expectations of the other person which block our ability to see them clearly.

The founder of this unique way of relating to the other person was an Austrian Jew by the name of Martin Buber whom Assagioli came to know and respect. Born in Vienna in 1878, Buber was undoubtedly influenced by the break up of his parent's marriage when he was three years old. Going to live with his grandfather's family at such an early age must have had a far reaching impact on his young mind.

An enthusiastic scholar by nature, Martin Buber went on to teach Philosophy at the Hebrew University in Jerusalem from 1939 to 1951. He was also very involved in the revival of Hassidism, a philosophy of loving kindness. Although embedded within Judaism, it was more mystical in nature and concentrated on the longing for God, joy and love. Influenced by the esoteric aspect of relationship with God, he began to view all human existence in the form of relationship. These were the primary relationship of I with an object, or the *I-It* dynamic. *I-It* exists in our relationship with others when we want something from the other in the form of information or monetary exchange. It is also when we do not relate to them as a person or soul, but more as an object or 'it'.

The second type of relationship manifests when the primary word 'I' is connected to 'Thou'. This is when we see the person as a soul and a deeper connection is manifested. Buber believed the *I-Thou* relationship was uttered, spoken or experienced with the *whole* being. In contrast, the *I-It* relationship was unable to communicate with the whole being because it only related to part of a person.

Buber held that these areas of relationship were responsible for our understanding of the world and each other. Dynamically, if the *I-Thou* relationship was utilized to address man, nature and art, which he had also studied at degree level, it would call for a spiritual dialogue.

Buber believed that within every encounter there was the potential for relationship and this was as much in the silence as in the words. True dialogue and meeting with the 'other' happened within the silence and between the words. Furthermore, he asserted that relationship was a two-way dynamic process. He wrote, *Let no attempt be made to sap the strength from the meaning of the relation: relation is mutual.*

So relationship is mutual, even in the silence.

Perhaps we can understand this when we have experienced silence in a room full of people which, in a positive sense, can be both moving and freeing. In contrast, silence can be uncomfortable, unbearable even, when thoughts are held in at some committee or business meetings. For a few moments, think about what silence holds.... How uncomfortable it can be and how we want to fill it with words, anything.

Now, think about the other kind of silence, the silence that is healing, empathic and embracing.

Within these different silences exist the *I-It* relationship which is uncomfortable, unbearable, so that we want to move on to change the energy. In contrast, the energy of the *I-Thou*, which engages our whole being, makes us reluctant to leave and break the spell.

How do we cope with challenging and uncomfortable silence?

Most of the time, in the workplace, we hold it in, don't say anything. And yet if we were to carry this through to a Right Relations group in psychosynthesis, we would struggle with it by bearing the discomfort. Anger and tears might be expressed as the silence breaks down and we defend ourselves against intimacy, that perilous *I-Thou* relationship. But something deeper would be allowed to emerge as someone 'voiced' what was held in the discomfort. And emerging through this there would be a sense of Thou and the other 'I'.

In our Western understanding of spirituality, this is not unlike the Quaker tradition where communication is spontaneous and arising from the silence, when one feels moved to speak. Having explored this area a little over the years and spoken to Quakers themselves there does appear to be a strong sense of 'Thou' in the room, and this can be understood as the 'I' attempting to dialogue with the 'Thou' present in the group.

As dialogue can exist in the silence, in the places between words, within any group of people, whether familiar or unfamiliar, this can be frightening and overwhelming unless it has a framework and a goal in the form of self-help. The age we live in is sometimes referred to as the 'Age of Aquarius' and we can understand this through the vast amount of networking and groups that exist in the world of cyberspace. There are groups for almost everything.

In therapy, the dynamic between the therapist and client is a dyadic one, like the parent and child. As in any dyadic therapeutic relationship, there are issues of regression and domination.

Both the Right Relations groupwork and Forum used in the training are unique to the Institute of Psychosynthesis where I trained.

### The Right Relations Group
The Right Relations group is made up of about 12 participants, sometimes referred to as a family constellation. This group meets three times a year over a full weekend. The group is anchored by someone well trained and familiar with the group processes which can manifest as the participants move through the various stages. It goes without saying that there is total confidentiality in the group and outside it. Many of the dynamics that individuals may have experienced historically in the family of origin will

reassert themselves in the group which can be challenging at times, although awareness of this will be helpful in the development of a stronger and more empathic individual. Each year, throughout the training, the Right Relations group will change with its new tool bag of opportunities. It is important to stress here, as in all group work, that there is just as much energy held in the silence as in the words. If anything holding the silence, feeling powerless and unable to speak, is just as challenging as speaking out in a large group.

*Forum*

In psychosynthesis, Forum is the name for the still larger group where everyone is invited to participate. This larger group can consist of some 40 or 50 members which is symbolic of society. The group meets for two hours every training weekend, or about once a month. On one level, the group dynamics can be regressive as one struggles with often overwhelming feelings of anxiety and helplessness, and yet on another level it is a gateway for transpersonal energies to break through as the will-to-good is activated. As one suffers the pain of the regressive feelings, there is a growing consciousness of ourselves and that within us which needs to be healed. Additionally, the transpersonal may bring up fear in us as well as love as we wrestle with the dilemma of making significant changes in our life. Recognizing our will to good can be just as unnerving as discovering our helplessness and fear. The realization of our potential can evoke a strong sense of responsibility and, yet, also a need to repress the sublime because we are afraid of both failure and success. Many of the issues arising in this larger group mirror the current issues in society. For example, if the country is at war or there have been bomb scares, starvation or earthquakes affecting thousands of people, Forum, like a lens, will focus in on these areas.

The experience of Forum will also heighten a need to belong and, paradoxically, a need to escape and run away from responsibility. These feelings can be tribal and overwhelming but they bring us the group experience of what it is to take responsibility for our lives and yet also feel alienated. This understanding in group relationships is an invaluable training ground for the therapy room. Unless the therapist has experienced and lived through ambivalent feelings, how can they ever hope to understand what is going on in the client?

It might be interesting to take a little time out to explore how you yourself experience relationships. Are you are aware of the difference between the *I-It* and *I-Thou* dynamic within yourself?

Can you remember when you experienced the *I-Thou* relationship in your life?

Closing your eyes, can you remember what brought it on and who or where you were? Have you experienced this with other people? or with an animal? or in nature?

You might want to make a note of these feelings and observations.

When we fall in love with someone this is often an *I-Thou* experience. We fall in love with the 'Thou' in the other person. We may first experience this when we first look upon the wonder of a baby, even if it isn't our own.

Reaching the end of this chapter, meditate for a few moments on these words of Martin Buber's: 'The *It* is the eternal chrysalis, the *Thou*, the eternal butterfly.'

Next, we explore the will. This includes personal will, skilful will and transpersonal will. The will is another unique component of psychosynthesis as Assagioli believed that there was an intimate relationship between the will and the Self. We look at where our will becomes trapped and how we can free it to do what our soul invites us to do.

# CHAPTER 7

## A Psychology with a Will

Our understanding of the will in the West is very much as an assertive and masculine energy which can be dominating, cold and overpowering. We often see a person as either strong-willed or weak-willed, dominant and proactive or unassuming and receptive. We equate strong will with success, power, innovation and personal leadership. We judge ourselves harshly by the criteria of success and progressive movement forward. Up until the late 70s with the arrival of the feminist movement, women were kept out of positions of leadership, as this was regarded as the province of the male and his will. Female leaders such as Germaine Greer and Marilyn French, through their writing, challenged the dominant mindset of women being married to the housework and men being the sole breadwinners. If women had a career it was a 'calling', like teaching and nursing and the pay was low in comparison with men.

Despite the fact that psychology has been around for a number of years and many of its early innovators were men who linked it with the sciences, surprisingly, the will has not featured strongly in psychology. Of course, it helped to have a strong will to overcome difficulties, but the will was often regarded in a negative way as being under the duress of the unplumbed depths of the unconscious. Since nearly all Freud's clients were women and he was the main pioneer in psychology, it suited the public image in those days to have weak-willed women who were prone to neuroses and hysteria. Yet, most of Freud's research was based on women who were struggling to oppose societal injunctions of being weaker and supporting the man.

To get anywhere in life without being shot down or humiliated, women had to use *another* aspect of will which I shall come to shortly.

While Freud was carrying out his research into hysteria and neuroses, Roberto Assagioli was developing the theory of the will which he described as having both male and female qualities. Furthermore, he asserted, both sexes had access to the masculine and feminine aspects.

The masculine quality of the will he saw as the will to power, domination, and innovation. Yet, strong will without being tempered by the love-wisdom aspect could become cold, clinical and even cruel. In contrast, the feminine aspect of will was motherly, loving, creative, nurturing and receptive. Again, if the feminine aspect was not balanced with strong will, it could become over protective, emotional and self-sacrificing. Rather than harnessing one aspect to the detriment of the other, Assagioli believed we should endeavor to become more balanced.

Assagioli believed that, too often, people developed one quality of the will and shied away from using the opposite one because they found it too challenging. We can see this in the world where there are powerful individuals who, although dominant leaders, tend to be ruthless and even cruel. Similarly, there are others in the world today who tend to be very nurturing and loving, almost to their own detriment, preferring to self-sacrifice rather than use their will to engage masculine energies which create protective boundaries. In fact, one can see the more developed the will is in one area, the greater the challenge to harness the other less dominant aspect. To the hardheaded business man who, through his will to power alone, has created an entire empire of wealth and innovation, the love aspect will be almost threatening to his success because it would involve compassion and caring towards his employees. As a result, intimate and equal relationships may be impossible. For the strong male, it is easier to harness the will to power and develop another empire. Relationships, love, nurturing are beyond him. Because of this inability to develop relationships outside the business enterprise, the entrepreneur can be lonely and isolated. I am reminded here of the Dickensian story of Scrooge, the seemingly indomitable businessman who could not celebrate Christmas, give to the poor or have empathy for any other living being, and whose sole focus on his savings set him up for a huge wake-up call. It was through his psychic awakening to his true nature that he saw the error of his ways. But underlying this was the fact that insight into his true nature opened his heart to such a degree that he began harnessing the feminine aspect of his will so that he became empathic, compassionate and deeply regretful of his ways.

Similarly, the person who is highly creative and tremendously resourceful with innovative ideas often lacks the self-confidence and will to market the ideas they have and see them through to completion. The fear of failure is too strong, or there is a lack of will to implement these activities. Additionally, they may find boundaries difficult for the fear of being labeled aloof and uncaring. Often, behind an extreme behavior pattern there is an all consuming fear of humiliation or loss. In the story of The *Christmas Carol* it would be interesting to work with his Scrooge character through subpersonalities where the need for money replaced a longing to love and be loved.

From referring to the table of male and female qualities are you able to see the masculine and feminine qualities within you or know which predominate?

| Masculine qualities | Feminine qualities |
| --- | --- |
| Will | Love |
| Logic/linear thinking | Creative/Abstract thinking |
| Authority | Service |
| Strength | Flexibility |
| Assertion | Receptivity |
| Power | Humility |
| Leadership | Relationship |
| Domination | Surrender |
| Expansion | Retraction |

It might be helpful to write some of these qualities down in a journal, listing the qualities of the masculine and feminine aspects of will and also the weaknesses in the form of fears which block the expression of these qualities. Making notes, asking questions, grounds and opens up insights that may not have been conscious before. In a few months, you might want to look at the journal and make another note of changes that have emerged within yourself since that first exercise.

Although we may have an idea about our strength of will, sometimes we can be totally thrown out of kilter when we find ourselves in an unknown situation which threatens our very sense of self.

Have you been in a terrifying or life threatening situation where you have come into contact with a part of yourself that, up until then, you didn't know you possessed?

Allow yourself, if you will, to return to that experience and reconnect with that feeling and make a few notes.

Ask yourself where that part of you has gone? Do you own it with pride or refuse to give credit for it out of fear? The fear that may come from having to live up to your potential.

I am reminded of a book I read a number of years ago called *Touching the Void* which reveals a harrowing mountaineering expedition by two climbers in the Peruvian Alps. They had planned to tackle the West side of Siula Grande with its sheer vertical face. Joe Simpson, after slipping down an icy crevasse suffered a compound fracture of the femur and patella. The other climber, Simon Yates was gradually lowering Joe down the side of the mountain when the rope got stuck. At this point, he was faced with a difficult choice as he didn't know whether Joe was safely on a ledge or dangling from the side of the mountain. Joe couldn't climb up because of his broken leg and Yates couldn't climb down because his belay ledge was crumbling. Furthermore, Joe had given no indication that he was alive and had failed to respond to his calls. The weight on the end of the rope was crippling and Yates knew it was only a matter of time before his own strength gave out and Joe would fall anyway. He had no choice but to cut the rope. Rather than them both dying, at least one of them would survive. Yates could have collapsed into exhaustion and despair, lost consciousness and died but it was the sheer force of his will which helped him make clear decisions when time was running out for them both. Miraculously, although Joe suffered a 100ft fall, he survived for four days by drinking drops of melting ice when crawling back to base camp just hours before Yates had planned to leave, assuming he was dead.

This demonstrates the tremendous reservoir of power we have to draw from during a life threatening crisis. Until we are faced with a crisis, we may never be aware of our strength of will; the will to survive, to live, to reach that life goal above and beyond all odds. In this case, strong and skilful will is at work here and, quite probably, the transpersonal. The transpersonal is miraculous.

Assagioli's work on the will was extensive enough for him to have completed a book on it, *The Act of Will.* This was a guide to self-actualization and self-realization and the will underpins the very structure of Psychosynthesis. Assagioli believed that the will and the Self were intimately connected. Certainly this can be experienced when the will latches onto a cause or, on a personal level, creates a work of art or births an idea of value. With the activation of the will, energies are released from the Self that can carry one forward.

## Skilful Will

Skilful will comes more easily to women and children although, in a less developed state, can be manipulative rather than skilful. Manipulation is based purely on selfish desire, whereas skill focuses on the situation rather than making it personal.

Strong will is rarely enough on its own to deal with the many situations in life that face us. When dealing with a stubborn child who is very engaged with finding their own strong will, some degree of skill is needed to take the child's mind away from the immediate object of his desire. In the first instant, we need to let go of our end of the rope which is causing the tug-of-war dynamic between the child and ourselves and add another element to the situation. This isn't giving in to the child's desires, because then the child will quickly learn that by exerting their will they can get exactly what they want. It is actually about bringing in another element, like a visit to the park or postponement which, if backed up by a valid reason why it isn't possible to do what they want now, they can have gratification later. In this situation the response needs to be fairly immediate. Most of the time, the child will accept the explanation and settle for delayed gratification instead.

But – what about that overgrown garden that we've been wanting to tackle since moving in three months ago!

The overgrown garden which is very open to postponement of any kind, requires a different skill. Strong will might be enough to engage us in a spurt of raw physical energy which quickly overwhelms us and put us off altogether. Half the garden may be tackled, but blistered hands and aching limbs take away some of the sense of achievement or even wanting to finish the job.

Instead, we might want to deliberate, which is one of the early qualities of will, then plan out our method of tackling the garden. For instance, we might decide to divide the garden up into manageable stages which we can set about doing over a period of weeks or days. Often the feeling of being overwhelmed accompanies something we want to tackle all at once. The same can be applied to a New Year's resolution of getting fit or losing weight. Because our initial goals and expectations are too high, we have set ourselves up to fail. In realizing the goals that are worthwhile and possible, we guarantee a greater sense of achievement.

Dieting is another will teaser!

And it is the difficulty in losing weight, the lack of self-control, that underpins the dieting industry. It is big business, costing billions and billions every year. Not all diets suit everyone and coupled with variability in metabolism according to age and temperament, losing weight is often an ongoing battle. Beginning with small manageable goals like cutting back on night time snacks has a greater sense of achievement. Instant crash diets, although involving strong will, very rarely last even though weight might have been lost. Unless we change our eating habits on a permanent basis, the weight will pile back on again. Without planning and deliberation, we can become quickly disillusioned. One thing we have to bear in mind is anything worthwhile takes time. Last minute revision might scrape us through an exam, but to really learn and utilize our long term memory we have to understand the ground of what we are learning, rather than concentrating on just the questions and answers.

Casting your mind back, can you think of anything that you have achieved through the use of skilful will?

If so, write it down and re-experience the feelings you had at your achievement. One of the things you will probably remember is the flow of energy you experienced when you set it in motion, giving you the motivation to begin. Often the inertia we experience is the energy we allow to get caught up in unconscious processes where our will is trapped.

Perhaps you can think of a project you have been wanting to do for a long time and begin to set down how you will achieve it and, by the process of deliberation, plan the steps to the goal and how to go about implementing it.

Assagioli believed that there were six distinct stages in willing from intention to realization. These are:

- Goal – purpose – intention – evaluation
- Deliberation
- Decision – Choice
- Affirmation
- Planning
- Direction of the execution

*Good Will*
Assagioli believed that as human beings we are in a continual state

of 'becoming' more of our authentic self. Embedded within this is the will to good and empathy for others, instead of criticism and judgment. Assagioli defines empathy as 'the projection of one's unconscious into another's being.' We are able to put ourselves in another's position and feel as they do. At this level the heart is activated and we want to do something to help alleviate the suffering. At the deepest level we may do something anonymously and receive no physical reciprocation other than knowing we have been of use to others in need. The purity of intent comes from not seeking recognition.

The recognition of global disaster through the visual media arouses a genuine humanitarian effort to alleviate suffering, poverty and suffering. Due to the instant relay of information globally, we are quickly alerted to disasters taking place in the world. Visual images engage us often on a soul level and this was the case affected by the Sumatran tsunami in 2004, the hurricane which destroyed New Orleans, and also the recent Earthquake in Haiti, all of which activated a mass outpouring of energy and goodwill to help in the immediate aftermath of the disaster.

One of the most moving acts of goodwill came from Charlie Simpson, a young seven year old boy in the UK who was so upset by the devastation wrought by the earthquake that he burst into tears on his mother's lap and told her he really wanted to do something to help. Together, they discussed what he could do and he decided to raise £500 for Unicef's Haiti appeal by riding his bike five miles around his local park. Incredibly, the young boy's vision raised £60,000 in just 24 hours. Also, the mother's genuine willingness to support her seven year old son in his vision is commendable. It makes me wonder how many other young people perhaps felt a similar will to good but did not have the understanding or time from supportive guardians.

Are you aware of a will to good in you?

Where in your body do you experience it?

When was it last active? Did you implement it? Why not?

Can you remember experiencing a will to good as a child? What was the incident? How were you met by this by carers?

## The Transpersonal Will

Trans-personal means, literally, 'beyond the personal'. For many, it represents the spiritual strand in our relationship with the world and each other. It is that 'something more' beyond the mundane. Experience of this can initiate an invocation of transpersonal qualities like 'falling in love' with a person, a venture or adventure, that 'more than' feeling which sets us on a quest to find the source of that quality. On a less positive note a transpersonal experience may evoke psychosis where one can feel frightened, terrified even. This can particularly happen to people who may not have developed a strong enough sense of 'I' or are emotionally and mentally fragile. For people who are mentally fragile or have been involved in drug experiences that undermine the ego stability, the superconscious energies may become messianic. The ego inflates and the person feels they have a special message to share with mankind. This is not to say that transpersonal experience is unreal... it is perhaps realer than real. But if the self collapses into these overwhelming experiences or visions and cannot synthesize them, they become split off which is often what schizophrenia is about. In our culture at the moment there is no understanding of shamanic experiences and, more to the point, little understanding of them. It takes a very special person to harness these powerful feelings in themselves in a culture that condemns it. Sadly, with all the drugs that are available, especially the stronger psychoactive properties of marijuana, psychotic episodes are increasing in our modern world. This may be one reason why transpersonal experience is feared and we have no language for it other than 'mental dis-ease'.

As the blood brain barrier is in place to prevent poisonous substances entering the brain, there is a strong analytical mind which protects us a certain amount from psychic material which we cannot understand. Yet – at some point on our journey, the mind cannot give us the answers we need and we enter what is known as an 'existential emptiness' or a void. Assagioli gives an example of this when Tolstoy at the age of 50 had achieved success in his life through his writing, didn't have to worry about money and was happy with his wife, but he felt a deep emptiness which nothing in the world could assuage. He was in pursuit of something beyond the everyday mundane consciousness. He was looking for *meaning* and *purpose* and *value*, the three qualities which Psychiatrist, Victor Frankl, listed were key to a prisoner's ability to survive the horrific conditions of Auschwitz where he was incarcerated. In 1948 he wrote a book *Man's Search for Meaning* which highlights the importance of this. It is now one of the ten most important books in the USA. Frankl's observations were based on his study of prisoners and guards in the camp. He understood that if the prisoners found meaning in their degrading and harsh conditions, they would survive the experience, retaining their sanity and dignity. Meaning, purpose and value were the qualities that engage the will with the transpersonal.

Another instance of this was when Buddha as a young boy, shielded from suffering, managed to escape the confines of his sheltered home environment and, for the first time, stumbled upon old, ill and impoverished people. This set him on a lifelong quest to find the meaning of suffering, where he tried fasting and yoga with very little relief for his questing mind. He eventually sat under a tree and received enlightenment. To engage him on this lifelong quest, he possessed a strong will and the desire to find the meaning of suffering. He also had the patience and vision to seek enlightenment. In our fast moving world, where quantity and speed is honored to the detriment of finer qualities, patience is often overlooked. We need to *persist* in realizing our vision.

Similarly, in our lifetime, we reach a point where we ask ourselves what is this life for ? What else is there? There is a longing for union with something greater which some have translated as the 'Beloved'. Certainly there is a longing for this expressed through religion, but too often these transpersonal experiences are suppressed. At the root of the 60s psychedelic culture and drug experiences today, which includes alcoholism, is the longing for the transcendental.

What have been your experiences of the transpersonal will?

Did you have these transpersonal experiences when you were a child? How did you manage them? Was this a turning point in your life?

The next chapter looks at where we might be unconsciously captured by the collective imagination in the form of the media. It also explores how we can make use of imagery to activate plans in our life.

# CHAPTER 8

## The Use of Imagery

*Whatever you can do or dream you can, begin it.*
*Boldness has genius, power and magic in it. Begin it now.*
**Attributed to Johann Wolfgang von Goethe**

The use of imagery is a key part of psychosynthesis, which can be used as a tool to develop qualities within ourselves and bring consciousness to previously hidden areas of the psyche.

Although the implementation of the will, which we have been discussing in the last chapter, is conscious, the use of imagery is largely an unconscious process. We look at a poster or catch a disturbing newsflash on the television and our mind conjures up all sorts of associative pictures which hook back into personal and collective memories. Similarly, our recent internalized imagery in turn can be projected onto our environment and the people we come into contact with. Last night's dreams may elevate and disturb us when they break through from the unconscious. Yet thrown into the waking world of the everyday, we are assaulted and seduced by more images that pull us further and further away from our dream world. But suddenly a door swings open and we remember the dream that had eluded us before; we daydream and allow ourselves to be captured by its imagery…. until our senses are captured again by the media in the form of newspapers, glossy magazines, television. The temptations are endless, the seduction subtle as it is bold. Young people long to look like the airbrushed models captured in glossy magazines… If they wore that lipstick, used this perfume, had their hair done this way, they could be happier and more self-confident. The fashion industry with its chameleon images is a flight we can never catch. And yet most of us are tempted to catch it at some time or other.

As we get older and our looks fail us, we run after new creams, vitamins that will keep us young, our body youthful. The seductive machine of industry goes on and on, enveloping every aspect of our life, our children, our animals, our gardens and the houses we live in. The advertising world is both seductive and ruthless in its desire to have our money, our investment and our eternal homage to its wares. And yet it consists almost entirely of imagery which, even the strongest of us, find hard to resist when they nudge against our weaknesses.

It was Sigmund Freud's nephew, Edward Bernays, who made use of his uncle's psychological theories and applied them to Public Relations. He himself as a Jew, was greatly affected by the power of the masses and had a deep suspicion of emotional libidinal drives. Ironically, and perhaps unconsciously, his advertising was a means of controlling the unleashed power of the masses and directing it towards an almost addictive desire to have 'objects' that would make them feel better. And this is why advertising by its use of imagery and appealing to our lack of emotional fulfillment is so successful today.

We live in a conscious world but, like the spring bulb that grows into a beautiful daffodil, we are still rooted deep in our unconscious. By becoming more conscious and using our will, we have the ability to decide what we want to be affected by.

Until we realize that we have little resistance against the onslaught of images waiting to beguile us, we collapse into a collective trance which the commercial world is modeled on. But the key to autonomy over the images that assault us hourly, daily is allowing that observing part of us, the 'I' to become conscious of this. Also, remember the power of questions. Questions jolt us out of the collective trance we tend to fall into because they force us to think and use the concrete part of our brain, rather than the abstract part. Questions, literally, make what is unconscious conscious.

What media images do you allow yourselves to be beguiled by? Have you been hooked into ones recently, even today?

What are they? What is the specific weakness they prey on?

Have these images left you feeling empty and inadequate? Or have they inspired you?

Write down how they have made you feel.

Assagioli's work with the imagination was influenced by the insight of Charles Baudouin, a Swiss psychoanalyst with an interest in autosuggestion, who suggested 'Every image has in itself a motor-drive.'

This is why we sometimes feel compelled to act when we see images, especially ones that are highly visual and are accompanied by auditory words as on television. Like all things this works in a positive sense as well as a negative one. Distressing disaster images evoke empathy and compassion and we feel compelled to make a contribution in whatever way we can. We imagine what it is like to lose our home, our family and we have to *do* something.

I am writing this in the wake of the Haitian earthquake in Port-au-Prince which took place in January 2010. Yet, despite the shortfalls of the media's insatiable obsession with celebrity and negativity, the speed at which full scale coverage of a disaster area and the needs that arise from this is equally commendable. As the scale of the earthquake filled our televisions, and distressing scenes of the dead, the dying, the trapped escalated, help in the form of money, service workers and the Armed Forces came pouring in from both poorer countries and wealthier ones. Everyone wanted to help and alleviate the pain and suffering in whatever way they could. Candles were lit in churches. If prayers could travel worldwide on prayer flags, the whole globe would be a dance of bright colours.

What impact do these incredible media images have on us as spectators from our comfortable homes? They open the heart and evoke the spirit of compassion within us. We experience the will to good. We are inspired to give, to help in whatever way we feel able. But on an even deeper level, we step out of the space we live in with its complexity of dissatisfaction, longings, sadness and irritability and occupy another more vibrant world. Good will begins to border on the transpersonal through the opening of the heart and emotions.

The opening of the heart allows us to feel grateful for our own circumstances, however tedious or problematic they may appear to be. We look around us with new vision and feel a sense of gratitude for what we have and, sadly, what we far too often take for granted. We are reasonably comfortable with food and all that we need, although maybe not with all that we want. In a material world that emphasizes the need for having more, owning more, becoming more, we can feel impoverished and lacking without really realizing it. If only we *were* more... or we *had* more or we didn't have this illness, this malady... And yet if we can be grateful for all that we have, including ailments and problems which never seem to go away, something happens in our hearts. Something invisible grows within that well of gratitude and we experience a sense of union with the world and that deeper part of us which it is often hard to stay connected with. Within this ambience of gratitude emerges grace, which is sadly absent in our culture of more, yet very present in poorer communities of less. Grace although present all the time is most visible and tangible in the presence of gratitude.

It is ironical that in our culture, where the media feeds into our insecurities of not 'being enough' or 'having enough', its hidden side is to make us realize how much we actually have and what we can give!

Our capacity to enable, support and offer prayers in times of crisis is boundless, because it emanates from the heart which is the pure expression of Spirit.

I think this sums up so well how powerful images evoke an immediate motor response. For many of us, our day is shaped by the 'feedback' we receive from others which can heighten or knock our image of ourselves. If our self-image is based on constant positive refueling from others, as it often is in the young who are more malleable, it doesn't take much to knock us flat. A positive self-image evokes a feel-good factor whereas a negative self-image makes us depressed with the tendency not to believe compliments or take glib comments to heart.

We tend to believe imagery is solely the province of the entertainment industry. After all, computer games, DVD's and digital cameras enhance and provide much of our entertainment. It is ironical that computers which, until the last 20-30 years, were used solely for work and 'computing,' have become a screen for entertainment rather than work. But imagery *is* work. At least the conscious creation of images is work, because, like driving a car or learning to ride a bicycle, we need to create new neural pathways in the brain. If we are unable to see ourselves doing something, there is no motivation to do it. So often we hear the expression, 'I can't see myself doing it somehow.' Similarly, we may not be able to 'visualize' the task because our hearts and will are not in it. But, given an undertaking that engages our heart and mind, we can imagine ourselves doing it without difficulty.

Animal Scientist, Temple Grandin, who has been known as 'the women who thinks like a cow' has done more for autism and the humane treatment of animals facing slaughter than any other person in the United States.

No one could have such an understanding of autism than Temple Grandin, as she was diagnosed with autism at the age of one and later with brain damage. Yet, despite all odds, she went on to study and earned herself a PhD. She has authored five books on autism and her work with animals. What makes her contribution so compelling is that *she actually thinks in pictures*. Language came later and was a lot harder to learn. The other quality that emerges from her work with animals, having been responsible for designing apparatus which makes the animals' lives less full of fear and anxiety, is her empathy with the animals, her understanding of how their mind works. Empathy is not an emotional quality that has ever been equated with autism. Yet, concerning her work with animals, she writes:

'Visual thinking has enabled me to build entire systems in

my imagination. During my career I have designed all kinds of equipment, ranging from corrals for handling cattle on ranches to systems for handling cattle and hogs during veterinary procedures and slaughter... I value my ability to think visually and I would never want to lose it."

In fact, Temple Grandin lives in a world of images where she can pre-run designs in her imagination to see how they work; viewing her invention from every angle and perspective. This is both amazing and far superior to our way of working, yet also equating with a very well designed computer program. In cognitive therapy, which is an effective way of treating anxiety disorders, imagery is becoming a key part of transformation and healing. This is called 'rescripting' where clients are invited to rewrite the script in the form of positive imagery in order to replace redundant negative past imagery.

It is interesting that the very things we want to do in life are thwarted with psychological obstacles which sabotage our will. Obstacles can be lack of confidence and the fear of public humiliation. These fears rarely go away by themselves. It is a matter of 'feeling the fear and doing it anyway' as Susan Jeffers proclaims in her book of the same title. But this isn't a matter of boldly going out into the public arena and just hoping for the best without any preparation or training. By doing this, unless we were very lucky, we would fulfill our deepest fear. We would fail.

To be able to see ourselves doing something is an act of visualization. As visualization is an exercise that involves the will, we need to train it regularly on a daily basis.

Using Temple Grandin's image work we can begin to apply this to the following exercise:

Think of a problem confronting you.

This can be a dilemma, a difficult choice that you feel you need to make. It might even be giving up something that you are too emotionally attached to and which is blocking the emergence of something more important.

At this stage, try not to define it in concrete terms.

Instead, just allow an image to come to you. Don't question the image or discard it and look for a more interesting one. Images are largely unconscious and it is because of this that we can harness and use the unconscious mind's expertise. Remember this is a dialogue between the unconscious and conscious mind. Remember also that the imagination is colorful, tactile, auditory and, in fact, deeply sensory.

Take your image, whether you can define it or not and turn it round in your mind. What does it look like from a different perspective? Does it open up or close down? What colour is it? Does it have a texture?

Reach out and feel it. Can you smell it or taste it. Is it old or new? Does it have soft and hard edges? Or both?

When you have explored all aspects of the image, ask it if it has a message for you. Try not to place limitations on it by getting it to conform to your expectations. Where would this image feel most comfortable?

Ground this insight by using crayons or pencils to draw the image and make notes about your dilemma. Do you have any feelings or thoughts around this? What are they? Ground this further by making a note of them?

You may find over the next few days that the image will keep popping into your mind to present different aspects of itself to you. Make a note of these too.

# CHAPTER 9

## The Use of Symbols and Exercises

*"Symbols as accumulators, transformers and conductors of psychological energies, and symbols as integrators have most important and useful therapeutic and educational functions"*
### Assagioli

Another powerful tool used in psychosynthesis is the use of symbols. These are often harnessed to find out what is happening in the unconscious mind.

### Words are symbols

As we begin reading a book, say a travel book, a good writer will immediately begin to convey images of foreign lands so that it impacts on all the senses. A book about Nepal will draw us into the dusty, hot streets of Katmandu where we can picture the rickshaws, see the colorful materials hanging outside the shops, and smell the array of spices that a stall holder has on display. A little later, in our imagination, we might find ourselves moving up the terraced rice fields past the shanty houses with the smell of burning reaching us from the wood fires and glimpse sight of the Annapurna mountain range. As we travel higher, the sounds and smells of village life drop away and we enter the stillness of the mountains, experience its cool air as the snowy ranges takes possession of our senses. The images, the writer conveys will with their 'motor effect' draw us in deeper as we become less identified with our immediate environment. Similarly, a writer who fails to evoke these powerful images will bore us and we become restless and irritable, turning our attention to something else. Images have to be powerful through the medium of the written and spoken word to tempt us into their world and sign up to their service.

Perhaps you can remember that time when, as a child, you made that transition from story books with pictures to ones without images. There would almost certainly be disappointment, a sense of loss. Certainly I experienced this and remember talking to other children who were feeling the same. We all thought we would never get used to what we called 'grown-up' books. But in time, our minds were creating internal images without really realizing it! In the adult world, images in a book are extra, like photographs the author has taken. But interesting covers sell magazines and books and these, beside the blurb on the back, ultimately encourage us to part with our money and join the world of consumers.

Every hour and day of our life, our conscious and unconscious minds are impacted on by symbols representing a mode of being. We use words so often that we forget they are original symbols. Words, written or spoken, evoke images which lead us into true or fictional stories. By following the words of a book, we are led into a complete narrative with characters, scenes worldly or otherworldly which evoke feelings and emotions within us. If we miss any part of the verbal or written tale, we lose important information which, like the piece of a jigsaw, gives us an ever emerging picture of something we can explore with our senses. Some words are more symbolic than others although all words are of equal value. Nouns on their own, for example: cat, house, car are very compelling. We can follow each of these nouns, open them up, and create or envisage their past, present and future history. Adjectives lend fluidity, movement or meaning in the format of inform-ation'. We live in a world of Information Technology (IT), meaning the information is forever 'coming into form.' Today, when IT dominates our personal and public life through computers, televisions, mobiles and musical systems, we can almost see it all coming into form.

The world of IT is escalating to such a degree that we are no longer waiting for a product to arrive; rather we are struggling to keep up.

For children, semantic symbolism is both powerful and colorful. As we grow older and more individualized, we will be attracted to some symbols more than others. Teenage years will be fast, bold emotive, sexual, with dance, fashion, fast bikes, motor cars, music, football, and dreams. We will use the imagination to take us on a journey of travel, romance and enjoyable activities. Later, we understand how to censor our symbols as we learn that not everything is possible or achievable. In contrast, the symbols of the elderly will be more reflective, less orientated towards the future and present. Symbols of the past will create memories and awaken new insights.

## The Use of Symbols in Therapy

To understand what may be happening in the unconscious of a client, a therapist may, for example, introduce this symbol of an empty bowl. The client will be encouraged to visualize the symbol and see what emerges. Initially, they may not be able to see or hold the symbol easily in their mind because they are not used to the discipline of concentration. The 'monkey mind,' which flits from topic to topic and becomes easily bored, will try to get rid of the image by sabotaging the concentration. In contrast, another client with a colorful imagination may be able to visualize a veritable cornucopia of fruit or sweets or some other tempting objects in his empty bowl. What is empty yearns to be filled — to move from emptiness to content because that is what we are used to. In many types of meditation, particularly in the Buddhist tradition, disciples will be encouraged to switch off their monkey mind and bring the mind to bear on a single 'seed' word, like 'happiness', 'peace' or 'compassion.' This technique focuses the mind and the student learns to observe the process of his thoughts and, gently, rein them in to focus on the seed word again. Both of these techniques can invite the client to learn about the levels of concentration and how hard it is to maintain an image of emptiness. Similarly, another client may find it hard to keep control of an overactive imagination, where the mind behaves like a runaway race horse. Sometimes the therapist will use the runaway racehorse as a working symbol; encouraging the client to gradually calm and take control of the horse by focusing their will. This may take time but gradually, through practice, the client will experience a slowing down in their imagination. It is not that the imagination has stopped; instead the client is learning to control it, rather than being controlled by it. No skill, however unique and prolific, is any good unless the owner is in control of it. We can now understand that a certain amount of will is needed in the process.

Symbols may appear simultaneously without the prompting of the guide or therapist. A client may reveal in the therapy session that she has been seeing a wooden box in her mind. The symbol has appeared spontaneously and been repetitive in nature, persisting over several weeks. Symbols tend to hang around until they are acknowledged. The therapist, without trying to interpret this, may explore this further by asking questions like; how big is the box? How old is it? What feelings does she associate with the symbol when she sees it? Can she connect it with anyone in her past? Who? Gradually as questions are asked about it, the symbol may change because the questions in therapy will continue giving life to it.

Assagioli had found through his work with clients that by connecting with the rich world of symbolism, a process of inner integration was taking place. Additionally, he identified three main types of symbols. These were organic like nature symbols, human symbols, religious or mystical symbols.

I have listed here some of the more common symbols in use today.

**Nature symbols**
Island
Mountain
Earth
Fire
Water

Cave
Sea
Lake
Rose
Lotus
Fire
Rain
Jewel
Diamond
Sky
Stars
Sun
Moon
Rainbow
Tree
Cave

This list is by no means exhaustive. Feel free to add your own organic symbols here that hold meaning for you.

**Animal symbols**
Again I include the more popular ones.
Lion
Tiger
Horse
Dog
Cat
Elephant
Bear
Tortoise
Dolphin
Whale
Crocodile
Frog

Wolf

## Transformative symbols

All symbols are transformative in a sense, but these are deeply so because of the nature of the process the 'life form' undergoes; for example the butterfly which becomes a caterpillar, then a chrysalis before transforming into a creature with wings, capable of flight.

Butterfly
Dragonfly
Egg
Spider
Eagle
Dove
Snake
Unicorn
Dragon
Salamander
Hummingbird
Bat
Triangle
Pyramid
Square
Circle
Chalice
Boat
Door
Cross
Pentagram
Sword
Eye (all seeing)
House
Ring

Crown

## Human symbols
Father
Mother
King
Queen
Magician
Princess
Prince
Knight
Wizard
Wise old man/woman
Hero/heroine
Wizard
Darth Vader
Birth/death

## Manmade symbols
Bridge
Road
House
Vase
Sword
Candle
Door
Temple
Wall
Mirror
Lighthouse
Letters
Numbers
Spade

Stairs

Gate

Because symbols largely originate from the unconscious, they often emerge through the fabric of our dream life. If we can remember our dreams then we will find them full of archetypal symbols. Freud was interested in dreams and once wrote,'dreams are the royal road to the unconscious.' Jung also studied dreams and symbols. One of the insights he had was that a dream is never an end in itself. Dreams have an ongoing life so that several dream sequences can, like a cine film, run through our life Simultaneously. But, because we don't remember our dreams, let alone remember the context from which they emerge, we can be oblivious of this. Jung encourages us to make a note of dreams, and as they are written down, inscribed through the symbolism of words, they come to life. I have found this to be true for myself and it is rather amazing realizing that even dreams are ongoing and part of an organic process.

This organic process takes us to the next chapter which is about our relationship with the environment and how the environment itself is embedded within the cells of our body.

# CHAPTER 10

## Psychosynthesis and Ecopsychology

*Altruistic love is not limited to the members of the human family. It can also embrace all living things in the animal and vegetable kingdoms of nature. This inclusiveness is expressed in the Buddhist love for all living creatures, and by Saint Francis in his 'Song of the creatures'. One might say an increasingly conscious sense of this universal brotherhood is behind the growing trend toward the cultivation of harmonious relations with the environment. This is the higher and broader aspect of ecology.*
**Roberto Assagioli, The Act of Will**

It is obvious by reading this quote that Assagioli perceived his work as encompassing all creation. This must have been a breakthrough in psychology where self-development and healing seemed only to apply to humankind. In fact, Assagioli was including and echoing the voices of other thinkers such as William James and eco-philosophers before him such as John Ruskin and Richard Jefferies, author of *The Story of my Heart*, Thoreau and his work at Walden Pond in the United States.

Ecopsychology or eco-therapy, as this subject is better known today, actually emerged in the mid 1900's. It was the work of various thinkers, poets and writers who created the ground for ecopsychology to thrive. William James, a psychologist and philosopher, found nature 'indispensible to his creative life' and was to write an essay entitled *A Certain Blindness in Human Beings,'* where he described human nature, in general, as lacking in empathy for the plants and animals they share the planet with. He believed one of the clues to finding meaning in life was the ability to find the connections between all living creatures.

Carl Jung, Assagioli's contemporary, revealed his personal appreciation of nature and its ability to heal in his words 'Matter in the wrong place is dirt. People got dirty through too much civilization. Whenever we touch nature, we get clean.'

Later, in the 1990s, Theodore Rozack,, Professor Emeritus of History and counterculture at California State University, wrote *Ecopsychology, Restoring the Earth, Healing the Mind* with a foreword by the renowned Jungian Psychologist, James Hillman. It was a collection of work by compelling environmental writers, from fellow psychologists, philosophers and scientists such as Edward O Wilson, David Abram and Jane Goodall. They all concluded that the way humanity as a whole was exiling the natural world from its life was making children and adults ill. The Wilderness Camps in the States back this up; children and adolescents from dysfunctional and emotionally challenged backgrounds benefit greatly from a period of living in the natural environment and getting to know each other through work and dialogue. Wilderness Camps are successful in harnessing the hidden qualities within their clients by calling them away from an environmentally impoverished modern world.

In fact, the natural environment has also been key to the rehabilitation of victims of torture, as demonstrated by the Natural Growth Project run by the Medical Foundation, where psychotherapists work alongside torture victims on an allotment in Hendon. By tending their own plot and working in harmony with the seasons to see the cyclical pattern of life in the soul, from seed to blossom, they can begin to trust in their own natural process again. The compelling environmentalist teacher and activist, Joanna Macey, discovered through her therapeutic work that many people were suffering from unconscious grief in their bodies through environmental despair.

She discovered from her 'grief' workshops that many of her participants suffered from a deep environmental despair about what is going on in the world; the ecological disasters of rainforests being felled, more and more animals losing their habitat as well as indigenous people losing their homes. Because of this, there is a deep endemic sense of powerlessness which can display itself as anger or depression. Together with John Seed, the Australian environmental activist, she created the Council of all Beings, a collective mourning ritual that enables participants to work with deep grief from environmental disaster. This process is very freeing because unexpressed grief carried for a long time, like lead, poisons the system.

It was the late Norwegian, Arne Naess, who founded the phrase 'Deep ecology'. He defined this as radically different from shallow ecology which believes that humankind is outside or above the rest of the biosphere. Deep ecology and eco-philosophy regard all life forms as integral, part of a living web, all supporting each other. This is a spiritual philosophy that engages all life, much like Buddhism.

Do you see yourself in relationship with your natural environment?

How do you feel when you see images of the natural environment vanishing underneath the forces that drive the economy?

How do you cope with this sense of powerlessness?

I feel ecopsychology has a vital role to play in modern psychosynthesis, not only because Assagioli must have envisaged this, but because it is a natural from of synthesis with a part of us that has been fragmented for too long. There are numerous examples where people who are mentally and emotionally fragmented through war and abuse heal in the presence of nature.

Next, we look at a model of psychosynthesis counseling and how this might move from the initial interview with a client, to the middle and end phase of counseling, to the dilemmas and insights waiting embedded within each stage.

# CHAPTER 11

## Psychosynthesis Counseling

### Initial Interview

All counseling begins with an initial interview so that counselor and client can begin to explore their relationship with each other, together with the work that may be involved. The interview lasts an hour and at the end of it a mutual decision will be made, whether the counselor is able to help the client and, in turn, whether the client feels that the counselor and the therapy is right for them.

Since most impressions are made in the first few minutes of contact, the client will know instinctively whether they can work with the therapist in the future. After all, this is going to be a relationship which may extend from six weeks to six months, a year or even longer. Most counselors will have had regular counseling themselves in the few years they have been in training. In fact, they may have had counseling for many years before considering training themselves. It is not uncommon for people who have undergone emotional and mental trauma themselves to want to train in an area that they know and want to help others in the same way that they have been helped.

### *Presence*

At all times during therapy, the counselor will be holding the transpersonal dimension of their work together. The counselor does not hold the tenet that her client is sick and needs to be healed as this, in a way, maintains this mental construction. If we believe someone to be sick then it is hard to change that belief or way of seeing the person. Instead, the counselor sees her client as having all the means to transform and heal herself. She sees that her existing problem or difficulty is because something is struggling to emerge, like the first snowdrops in winter. Because she accepts this as part of the transformative process, she is able to hold this for her client too. Her presence, which is so important in their work together, is one of Unconditional Positive Regard and respect for the person before her. 'Unconditional positive regard' is the term Carl Rogers, the founder of Humanist psychology, used to describe the therapeutic relationship.

Because the client may have vacillated about therapy for some time, there may be a lot of tension in the room and the client feels they have to talk in order to fill the empty space. The counselor will put the client's mind at rest by simply asking, 'How do you feel about being here today?' This gives an opportunity for the client to pan back to her original reasons for coming and release some of the inevitable nervous tension in the room. It also gives the therapist, through attentive listening, the opportunity to begin to form an impression of her client by the words she used to describe herself and her life.

In order to draw up a plan for the therapeutic relationship, she will need the client to give her the following information.

- Historical background,including family and important parental figures.
- Any issues or traumas that may have arisen as a result of this.
- Medical background.
- Emerging issue: What brought her to therapy?
- Has she had counseling before? What worked and what didn't work?
- The client's expectations and fears.

The emerging issue might not be apparent until the counselor asks the client what has brought her to therapy and what her fears and expectations are.

It might seem strange, but even the most intelligent person can have a complete blind spot as to how they come across to others, or even what their problems or problem are although it may be obvious to everyone else. The client may start with, 'I just can't seem to get anything right lately' or 'Everything I do seems to fall apart…

Nothing seems to work… I'm just useless.'

As there seems to be an issue with low self- esteem, the counselor will ask if the client is depressed. And if they are, how long they have been depressed?

The realization that they might be depressed might come as a shock to the client and they will withdraw a little to let this sink in, or the client may be defensive in order to block this knowledge.

Then the counselor, after defining what psychosynthesis is and how it works, will brief the client on what their future work will involve if she is still interested. She will suggest a set of six sessions held over the same amount of weeks. This will give structure and direction to the work. In some cases only six weeks may be needed to determine a course of change and action. For others, where there may be deep rooted historical issues that are impeding their ability to reach out or find the will to implement important changes in their life, it might take longer. If the client has been in therapy before, this may have an impact on their future sessions together. I can illustrate this by giving an example here.

*Counselor*: You mentioned you had therapy before. Can I ask how long this lasted? And what sort of therapist you saw?
*Gemma*: Psychoanalysis. I was in it several years. It helped me deal with a lot of childhood stuff, with my father and how I was still affected by it.
*Counselor*: Can you tell me why you left?
*Gemma*: Well – I just felt we weren't getting anywhere. I knew why I was like I was and I felt I'd come to terms with a lot that had happened in my childhood. But I didn't want to keep exploring. I just wanted to live my life.
*Counselor*: Mirrors her spread hands. *That sounds reasonable.*
*Gemma*: A short silence, which allows Gemma to collect her thoughts. *I read about humanistic counseling and I was torn between this*

*and Jungian psychology but then a friend told me about psychosynthesis and it sounded very creative.*

**Counselor:** *Creative?* The therapist amplifies the word, inviting further dialogue.

**Gemma:** *Yes. I used to write poetry when I was a child and paint but I let it go.* She smiles suddenly at the counselor *I'd like to reconnect with that part of me again.*

**Counselor:** *You'd like to reconnect with your creativity?*

**Gemma:** Nods enthusiastically and suddenly a smile lights up her face.

This is the initial interview and if the client and counselor feel they want to work together, the counselor will make an appointment to see her in a week's time. She will probably suggest that Gemma starts writing a biography about herself if she hasn't already. This helps her to be open to how her history impacts on the present, grounding her observations and making sense of what is going on inside her alongside the therapeutic relationship.

### The Beginning and Bifocal Vision

Everything has a beginning, middle and an end.

But within this context, the counselor will be using what is known as *bifocal vision*. This is a technique that Assagioli devised in order to determine what is foreground and background in the therapy session. In this case, using the example of the session with Gemma, we would see that in the foreground she is wanting to become more creative by reconnecting with her artistic abilities as a child. Since this is a transpersonal psychology, the counselor will be holding this in the background, in the form of spirit and soul.

At the beginning of this therapeutic alliance, as trust is created and communication between therapist and client reaches an optimum level, the client may experience a sense of euphoria; of everything being wonderful and new. Additionally, her dream life may have received a boost; becoming vibrant and colorful. The emotional and mental restraints that she experienced prior to coming to therapy seem to have loosened. Instead, she experiences a freedom such as she has never known before.

But the counselor will be aware of this and realize that this is a brief honeymoon period built on trust and the powerful dreams for the future. The counselor will also be aware that because her client has entered the field of transpersonal energy and is beginning to experience a newfound confidence, she is in touch with the superconscious. She will gradually begin to build helpful psychosynthesis exercises into their sessions. The first and main one being the identification and dis-identification exercise which is helpful to centre the mind, body, and emotions. Other exercises may be creative ones where pen and paper are used to ground insights that are beginning to emerge.

Gently, the counselor will remind her client of the plan she had initially wanted to draw up; that of being 'more creative' and will begin to direct her vision towards the future as a way of bringing the thought down into matter. The counselor and client may perhaps find that this 'toying' with dreams, rather than bringing them into form, may be a pattern that Gemma uses in order to avoid disappointment and failure or even success. While ideas and dreams are not fledged and in a free floating form, there is no real commitment to carry them forward into matter.

There may be areas they both want to explore with subpersonalities.

For example, Gemma may have a strong dreamer who prefers to engage her energy in a fluffy world. Once Gemma has identified with this aspect of herself, the counselor invites her to give this part of her a name. This makes the work real. In this case, we will call her 'Cindarella,' who dreamed of being whisked away in a carriage to a wonderful banquet by a fairy godmother. Exploring further, the therapist will help Gemma uncover what this subpersonality is protecting. Usually these sorts of fairytale figures in the form of princes and knights in shining armor, are protecting something very vulnerable. Maybe, through further exploration and visualization, the Cindarella subpersonality is protecting a young child from being hurt and wounded. It is ironical that the nearer you get to the core of a subpersonality, the nearer you get to the Self.

## Middle Therapy

Once the middle ground is reached in the therapeutic relationship, the honeymoon period is over. The client, through their work with subpersonalities, has a stronger sense of themselves. Furthermore, through a stronger sense of 'I,' the will is more active and there will be less of a sense of things happening to them as Gemma starts to exert a greater autonomy over the conditions of her life. Emerging from this will be a deeper sense of identity.

With the therapist's encouragement, Gemma will be able to take risks in her relationship with the therapist in being more authentic about her needs and wishes. In turn, the therapist will encourage her client to make the decisions about what she wants to cover in their sessions together. If her confidence wavers and she regresses to an earlier state, the therapist will be able to see that this is in the service of something that is struggling to emerge and will support her in this. If the therapy is going round in circles, she will bring Gemma's attention to the needs and wishes she had expressed early on in their therapy. Because of the transpersonal element of psychosynthesis, the therapist will need to check out from time to time how she perceives this context. Does she look upon the transpersonal element as something that can save or rescue her and make things cosy or an influence that is guiding her and working with her. This distinction is important as it determines her ability to take control of her life more fully.

## The End

Endings are never easy in relationships because they activate powerful contradictory emotions in the therapist and client. These emotions will go back to a very young age and always there is the fear of the unknown, existential loneliness and regret. The therapist, like a mother, will fear for the safety and future welfare of her client. Can she trust enough to let her client go without necessarily reaching a happy ending? The client too may feel herself regressing as she seemingly loses the support of someone she has come to trust and possibly love. In the therapeutic relationship, strong feelings are invoked of love and abandonment. The client may defend herself against the pain of loss by asking if they can keep in touch by telephone and email from time to time. However well their relationship went, this should not be encouraged, because this is prolonging the inevitable and can possibly activate an earlier dynamic of not being able to let go in a relationship.

An experienced therapist will be aware of all these issues and realize how important it is that during these last sessions together they re-evaluate the journey the client has made and where she sees what she has learned/ gained will serve her in the future. Questions like 'Where do you see yourself fitting into society?' or 'What things will you do to activate your dream of being creative?' and 'What courses are you going to do?' will play an important role here.

Some endings may be messy and unfinished.

The therapist might become sick or home circumstances may cause her to fold up the therapy without much warning. The client may be thrown back on themselves, and forced to dig deeply to find resources within her to cope with this sudden loss. Alternatively, this 'unfinished business' with a significant figure may overlay other similar experiences of abandonment from her historical past – all of them painful. Patterns have a way of repeating if they have valuable lessons for us to learn. But this does not mean Gemma has to collapse into the loss. She can learn from this ending with an awareness that she can react differently this time. She can bring what she has learned to a new therapist and continue from there or take time out before considering this.

# GLOSSARY

**Collective unconscious:** Universal unconscious psychological material which we inherit on a group level.

**Countertransference:** The therapist's feelings towards the client.

**Esoteric:** Philosophical doctrine available to the initiate or the chosen few.

**False persona:** Development of a false self in order to be accepted or liked.

**'I':** The conscious self which makes decisions and choices.

**Id:** A term used by Freud to describe the instinctive part of us at birth who is full of needs.

**Intrapsychic:** Our internal psychological processes.

**Interpersonal:** Interactive people skills used to communicate with others.

**Object relations:** A psychological term used to describe relations between internal and external objects. We learn this in childhood and try to integrate this within ourselves.

**Peak experience:** Maslow described this as 'sudden feelings of intense happiness and well being'.

**Psychodynamic Theory:** A form of psychotherapy,based on Freudian analyses, to facilitate the emergence of unconscious material in the client.

**Self and self:** Self is equivalent to spirit. self represents the personality.

**Solar Plexus:** A nerve plexus where where we experience the 'flight or fight' response. Also a major chakra where we process emotional material.

**Soul:** That part of us which travels with us and incarnates into matter through the medium of the personality and body.

**Spiritual flight:** A tendency to detach from body, mind and feelings in the midst of emotional trauma and gravitate towards an idealized world in order to escape/cope with feelings of extreme discomfort and pain.

**Superconsciousness:** Higher consciousness through which we gain spiritual, visionary insights, often accessed through meditation..

**Superego:** A historical parental influence that carries a template of 'right' and 'wrong'.

**Transpersonal:** Beyond the personal. Spiritual experience or insight.

# BIBLIOGRAPHY

Alighieri, Dante, *The Divine Comedy*, Oxford Paperbacks, 1998

Assagioli, Roberto, *Psychosynthesis*, HarperCollins, 1993

Assagioli, Roberto, *The Act of Will*, David Platts Publishing Company, 1999

Benson, Jarlath, *Old Wine in New Bottles*, Year Two Course Book. Published by Amacara Press for the Institute of Psychosynthesis, 1992

Buber, Martin, *I and Thou*, Continuum books, New York, 2008

Chetwynd, Tom, *A Dictionary of Symbols*, Paladin, 1982

Grandin, Temple, *Thinking in Pictures*, Vintage Books, 2008

Hardy, Jean, *A Psychology with a Soul*, Woodgrange Press, 1996

Jung, Carl, *Memories, Dreams, Reflections*, Vintage 1989

Le Guin, Ursula, *Earthsea Trilogy*, Bantam 2006

Simpson, Joe, *Touching the Void*, Vintage New edition ,1998

Roszack, Theodore, Gnomes Mary, *Ecopsychology*, The Sierra Club Books, 1995

Tart, Charles, *Beyond Ego*, from the book *The Spirit of Science*, edited by David Lorimer, Floris Books, 1998

Whitmore, Diana, *Psychosynthesis Counseling in Action*, Sage Publications Ltd, 1998

# RECOMMENDED READING

Ferruci, Piero, *What we May be*, HarperCollins, 1995

Benson, Jarlath, *Working More Creatively with Groups*, Routledge, 2004

Russel Peter & Evans,Roger, *The Creative Manager*, Jossey-Bass Inc, publishers, San Francisco

Sorrell, Stephanie, *Depression as a Spiritual Journey*, O Books, 2009

**Useful Websites**

Stephaniesorrell.com/

http://www.aap-psychosynthesis.org/

http://www.psychosynthesis.org/

http://www.psychosynthesis.edu/

# BOOKS

O is a symbol of the world, of oneness and unity. In different cultures it also means the "eye," symbolizing knowledge and insight. We aim to publish books that are accessible, constructive and that challenge accepted opinion, both that of academia and the "moral majority."

Our books are available in all good English language bookstores worldwide. If you don't see the book on the shelves ask the bookstore to order it for you, quoting the ISBN number and title. Alternatively you can order online (all major online retail sites carry our titles) or contact the distributor in the relevant country, listed on the copyright page.

See our website www.o-books.net for a full list of over 500 titles, growing by 100 a year.

And tune in to myspiritradio.com for our book review radio show, hosted by June-Elleni Laine, where you can listen to the authors discussing their books.

MySpiritRadio